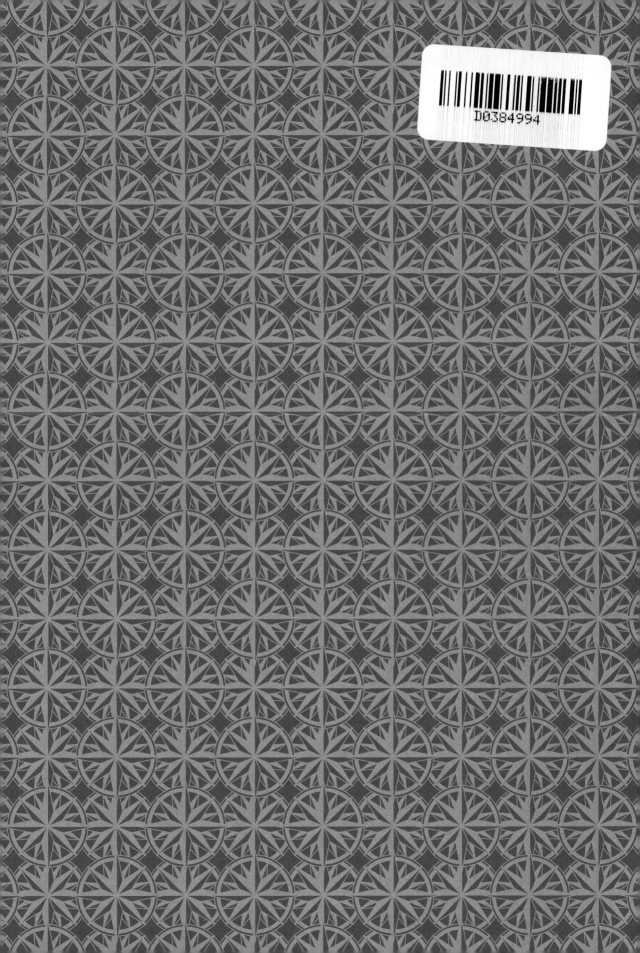

YANOMAMI HUNTER, BRAZIL

The forest is one big thing; it has people, animals, and
plants. There is no point saving the animals if the
forest is burned down; there is no point saving
the forest if the people and animals who live in it
are killed or driven away. The groups trying to save
the races of animals cannot win if the people trying
to save the forest lose; the people trying to save the
Indians cannot win if either of the other loses;
the Indians cannot win without the support of these
groups; but the groups cannot win without the help
of the Indians, who know the forest and the animals
and can tell what is happening to them. No one of us
is strong enough to win alone; together, we can be
strong enough to win.

PAIAKAN
Kayapó leader

Prepared by the Special Publications Division
National Geographic Society, Washington, D.C.

THE EMERALD

REALM
Earth's Precious Rain Forests

SUNSET, COSTA RICA

TRAILING ORCHIDS, MADAGASCAR

Emerald Realm: *Earth's Precious Rain Forests*

Contributing Authors: RON FISHER, TOM MELHAM,
CYNTHIA RUSS RAMSAY, PETER H. RAVEN,
JENNIFER C. URQUHART

Contributing Photographers: JOSÉ AZEL, MICHAEL
MELFORD, MICHAEL NICHOLS, GEORGE STEINMETZ

Published by
THE NATIONAL GEOGRAPHIC SOCIETY
GILBERT M. GROSVENOR
    President and Chairman of the Board
MELVIN M. PAYNE, THOMAS W. McKNEW,
    Chairmen Emeritus
OWEN W. ANDERSON, *Executive Vice President*
ROBERT L. BREEDEN, *Senior Vice President,*
    Publications and Educational Media

Prepared by
THE SPECIAL PUBLICATIONS DIVISION
DONALD J. CRUMP, *Director*
PHILIP B. SILCOTT, *Associate Director*
BONNIE S. LAWRENCE, *Assistant Director*

Staff for this Book
MARTHA C. CHRISTIAN, *Managing Editor*
CHARLES KOGOD, *Illustrations Editor*
CINDA ROSE, *Art Director*
PATRICIA F. FRAKES, *Senior Researcher*
ANN NOTTINGHAM KELSALL, *Researcher*
JULIE L. ESTES, *Research Assistant*
LESLIE B. ALLEN, RON FISHER, TOM MELHAM,
    GENE S. STUART, JENNIFER C. URQUHART,
    Picture Legend Writers
JODY BOLT, SUSAN I. FRIEDMAN, JOSEPH F. OCHLAK,
    Map Research and Art
SANDRA F. LOTTERMAN, *Editorial Assistant*
SHARON KOCSIS BERRY, *Illustrations Assistant*

Engraving, Printing, and Product Manufacture
GEORGE V. WHITE, *Director,* and
VINCENT P. RYAN, *Manager, Manufacturing*
    and Quality Management
DAVID V. SHOWERS, *Production Manager*
KEVIN HEUBUSCH, *Production Project Manager*
LEWIS R. BASSFORD, TIMOTHY H. EWING,
    Assistant Production Managers
CAROL CURTIS, KAREN KATZ, LISA A. LaFURIA,
    KATY OLD, DRU STANCAMPIANO,
    MARILYN J. WILLIAMS, *Staff Assistants*
BRYAN K. KNEDLER, *Indexer*

CUTTING MAHOGANY, COSTA RICA

Contents

BRAULIO CARRILLO NATIONAL PARK, COSTA RICA

Endangered

"We still know relatively little about the abundance of life in tropical rain forests. Amazingly, we know more—much more—about the surface of the moon."

by

Peter H. Raven, Director

Missouri Botanical Garden

The trees of these Indies are a thing that cannot be explained, for their multitude; and the earth is so covered with them in many parts, and with so many . . . dissimilarities between them, both in their great size as well as in the trunk and branches and bark and in . . . their fruit and flowers, that not even the native Indians know them. . . . In places one cannot see the sky from below these woodlands (for their being so tall, and thick, and full of branches). . . . GONZALO FERNÁNDEZ DE OVIEDO Y VALDÉS—1526

With Oviedo, I share the wonder expressed in his chronicle of the New World, but my wonder is coupled with frustration that even today we know relatively little about earth's

Realm

trees on Costa Rica's Osa Peninsula, the thought of the thousands of species of insects, plants, vertebrates, and fungi living their entire lives in the canopy above fascinated me. The occasional multihued parrot or large, iridescent-winged blue morpho butterfly sailing through a sunlit clearing accentuated for me the diversity and beauty of tropical rain forests.

Since then, I have spent much of my time speaking and writing about rain forests. Currently, as head of the Missouri Botanical Garden, I serve as an advocate for tropical forests around the world. In the 25 years since my early experience in Costa Rica, at least two-thirds of Central America's rain forests have been cleared. And the destruction has not been limited to Central and South America. Around the globe, tracts of these forests are being destroyed at an ever more rapid pace.

What rain forests are and where they occur, why they are disappearing and what we can do about it must be of concern to all of us if there is to be any hope of preserving these valuable and complex ecosystems.

Tropical rain forests are scattered in an uneven green belt roughly between the Tropic of Cancer north of the Equator and the Tropic of Capricorn south of it. They grow in regions where at least four inches of rain falls monthly, where the mean monthly temperature exceeds 75°F, and where frost never occurs.

Several subcategories of tropical forest depend on variations in terrain and rainfall. And not all rain forests are tropical. Some, such as those on the Olympic Peninsula in Washington State or in the Tongass National Forest in Alaska's Panhandle, grow in temperate zones. Unlike tropical rain forests, which have mainly broad-leaved evergreen trees, most temperate rain forests are made up of needle-leaved plants, or conifers. Biologically, temperate rain forests are much less diverse than tropical ones.

This book will deal with the lowland evergreen tropical rain forest—the richest, most biologically diverse community of living things on earth. For example, as many as 200 species of trees may be found in *a single acre* of tropical rain forest. In contrast, only about 400 species of trees occur in *all* of temperate North America. A single square mile of Amazonian Ecuador or Brazil may be home to more than 1,500 kinds of butterflies; only about 750 occur in all of the United States and Canada.

Tropical rain forests now cover less than 5 percent of the earth's land surface, but they are home to perhaps half of all the earth's species. Literally millions of species of plants and animals live together, interacting in the most complex ways imaginable. The great majority exist amid the layers of foliage, far above the rather open forest floor, rarely or never descending to the ground.

Estimates vary widely, but the truth is that no one knows how many species are in the tropics. Most of the vertebrates, butterflies, and plants have been discovered and named, but millions upon millions of other insects and microorganisms are still largely unknown.

In recent studies Terry Erwin of the Smithsonian Institution in Washington, D.C., obtained comprehensive samples of the insects found in tropical canopies. He and other scientists accomplished this by sending up fogs of insecticide and catching everything that came down. Their findings led them to estimate that the actual number of species of insects in tropical forests might be between 30 and 80 million.

In contrast, fewer than half a million tropical species of any kind have been cataloged. After *(Continued on page 18)*

Severd Falls plunges over a precipice in Peru as a light plane circles above. A national park protects the falls and the surrounding rain forest in the upper Amazon drainage, one of the most complex ecosystems on earth.

Competition for light and space never ceases here in a rain forest in Costa Rica. In tropical forests heat and humidity and frequent rainfall nurture a diversity of life-forms in four zones: the dim forest floor, the tangled understory, the dense canopy of broad-branched trees, and the emergent tops of the tallest trees.

Trailing mosses and spreading ferns bring a pervasive serenity to temperate rain forests in Oregon and Washington. Far to the north of the Equator, such moist woodlands—biologically not as diverse as tropical forests—thrive in cool coastal climates. Mushrooms springing up among mosses carpeting a stump draw nourishment from decay and reflect the interdependence of life in all rain forests.

Embattled tropical rain forests, shown in red, range round the globe. Identified by nation, these areas shrink daily as shifting agriculture and fuelwood gathering, ranching, mining, and logging encroach on them.

NORTH AMERICA

United States

ATLANTIC OCEAN

Tropic of Cancer

Mexico

Haiti

Dominican Republic

Cuba

Puerto Rico

Hawaii

Belize

Venezuela

Jamaica

Trinidad and Tobago

PACIFIC OCEAN

Guatemala

Honduras

Guyana

Nicaragua

Suriname

CENTRAL AMERICA

Costa Rica

Panama

French Guiana

0° Equator

Colombia

Ecuador

Amazon River

Peru

Brazil

SOUTH AMERICA

Tropic of Capricorn

Bolivia

Paraguay

Argentina

L ocated between the Tropic of Cancer and the Tropic of Capricorn, tropical rain forests once blanketed 12 percent of the earth's land. Now they have been reduced to only about 5 percent. Two leading characteristics of these forests are the nearly uniform climates in which they occur (a minimum of four inches of precipitation every month and a mean annual monthly temperature exceeding 75°F with no frost ever occurring) and their biological diversity. Forests of this kind exist at relatively low elevations, usually below 4,300 feet. The largest areas of such forest are in the Amazon basin of

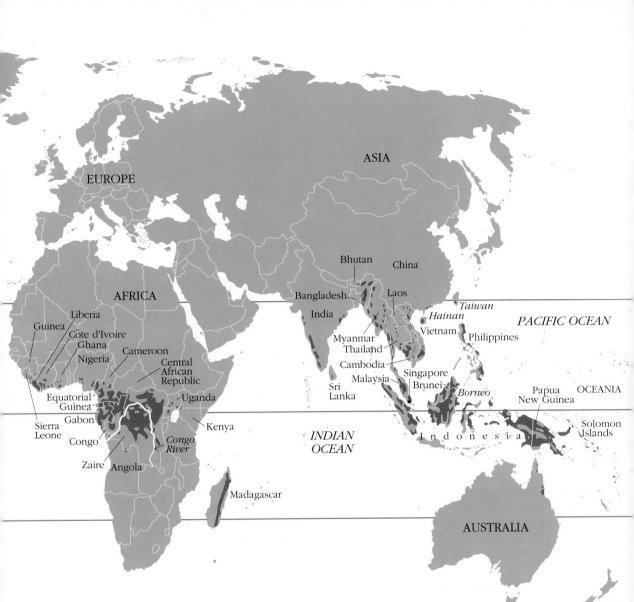

South America, with extensions into coastal Brazil, Central America, and Mexico, as well as some of the islands of the West Indies. In Africa rain forest occurs in the Zaire (Congo) basin and along the west coast of the continent. The third major area extends from Sri Lanka and western India to Myanmar (formerly Burma),

the Philippines, Malaysia, Indonesia, and northeastern Australia. Tropical rain forests consist of tall, evergreen, mostly broad-leaved trees. The branches of these trees tend to form many layers, each of which shelters a distinct array of creatures. Most of them spend their entire lives in the canopy and are rarely seen on the ground below.

decades of intense scientific study, we still know relatively little about the abundance of life in tropical rain forests. Amazingly, we know more—much more—about the surface of the moon.

Each species of the millions of rain forest organisms holds secrets locked in the code of its genetic makeup. Some few of these secrets have been discovered— enough to reveal that the rain forest is important to our future well-being. Particularly with the ability to transfer genes from one kind of organism to another, we must view the tropical forests as what one British ecologist has called "a sack of uncut diamonds," a priceless treasure of tremendous potential for humanity.

Each organism—from a giant tree hundreds of feet tall to a microbe on the forest floor that helps that tree live—has

made its unique adaptation to life. And the information encoded in its genes may have value for us humans, as we struggle to adapt to swift changes in our environment.

Genes from wild tropical strains of standard food-crop plants have already proved important in developing disease-resistant and high-yield crops. In medicine rain forest plants are a source of treatments for major diseases, such as cancer.

Time is now running out for the animals and plants of the rain forest. Every year, an area *(Continued on page 24)*

Following a serpentine course, the Mucajai River cuts through Brazil's Amazon region. Seemingly endless but rapidly decreasing, this forest covers much of the sparsely populated Amazon basin, an area roughly ten times the size of Texas.

COCK-OF-THE-ROCK

Bedazzling adornments and efficient forms suggest the long adaptation of animals and plants to their tropical habitats. Scientists estimate that half of all species live in rain forests.

DART-POISON FROG

PRAYING MANTIS (ABOVE); SIFAKA, RIGHT

Sinuous buttresses angle from a massive trunk. Trees growing on poor rain forest soil—leached by millennia of rains—have few deep roots. To absorb food from decaying surface litter, the roots of even lofty trees spread mostly horizontally. Buttresses may serve as supports.

roughly the size of Illinois is slashed and burned, logged, or otherwise destroyed, and at least an equal amount is disturbed. About half of the world's original tropical rain forest is already gone, with the remainder now covering an area only about the size of the 48 contiguous states of the United States. During the next 20 to 30 years, this will be reduced to scattered remnants, except for major patches in the northwestern and northern Amazon region of South America and perhaps others in the interior of Africa.

The most tragic and permanent effect of the disappearance of tropical rain forests is biological extinction. As the forests disappear, the number of extinctions will be greater than at any other time since the demise of the dinosaurs 66 million years ago. A quarter of all biological diversity in the world—more than a million species—is likely to vanish within the next quarter century. Before the secrets of the rain forest are unlocked, its gifts discovered, its treasures saved, it will be gone—unless steps can be taken now

to preserve as much of it as is possible.

Another major problem associated with the loss of forests is the greenhouse effect. Although the burning of coal, oil, and natural gas—the so-called "fossil fuels"—is the major contributor to the intensification of the greenhouse effect, the destruction of forests is estimated to contribute as much as a third to the total carbon dioxide, one of the primary "greenhouse gases." As the wood decays or burns, millions of tons of carbon dioxide are released into the atmosphere.

Like the panes of glass in a greenhouse, gases trap solar radiation, maintaining the earth at its present temperatures. As more gases are added, temperatures will slowly increase, with potentially

Trees leveled in Malaysia for export indicate logging's role in tropical deforestation. But when properly managed for sustainable yields, rain forests can supply abundant raw materials for industry as well as foods and medicinal plants.

serious consequences for the planet.

Stopping the destruction of rain forests has become a popular cause around the world—and for excellent reasons. However, the needs of ever increasing human populations, along with the political and social pressures caused by the unequal distribution of wealth, are complex forces. And these are the very forces that are causing the rain forests to disappear.

When Europeans arrived in the New World tropics, they began to convert forestland to ranches and farms. They started by clearing the tropical deciduous forest, because it grew on fairly good soil. But today, with the population explosion, settlers have turned to even very poor soils where most tropical evergreen forest grows. In these areas crops usually deplete the land within a couple of years.

We now know that the secret of luxuriant growth within an undisturbed rain forest is not in its soil. The soil is generally low in phosphorus and nitrogen—both of which are required by plants—or the soil is often highly acidic, which makes it difficult for plants to obtain nutrients. Plants in rain forests thrive generally by hoarding essential nutrients in their own bodies and then recycling them. When leaves, branches, or whole trees fall, they encounter a thick mat of roots that grow mostly in the top inch or two of soil. Some of the roots penetrate more deeply, but the majority are concentrated in the surface mat. These roots rapidly transfer nutrients from fallen organic matter back into the plants from which they came, and the cycle continues undisturbed.

But when large tracts of rain forest are cut for ranching or farming, the entire system of nutrient transfer is lost. In the beginning nutrients from the ashes of burned trees temporarily fertilize the soil, thereby enabling crops to grow well for a few years. Inevitably, though, the nutrients are used up, and crops grow only with difficulty. Unable to obtain essential nutrients, they fall prey to pests and diseases.

Like ranching and farming, logging is a primary cause of deforestation in the tropics. To harvest certain species of especially desirable hardwoods from tropical forests, where hundreds or even thousands of different species grow, it is often more profitable to destroy entire tracts of forest. And after the destruction very little reforestation goes on. On the average one tree is planted for every ten cut.

In fact, the forces at work against the survival of the rain forests are complexly political, social, and economic. Nations in the tropics assert their right to determine how to use *their* rain forests. At the most basic level well over half of the people in the tropics use wood as their primary source of fuel. At the national level governments struggling with poverty and high population densities see rain forests as a means of some immediate relief. Massive foreign debts often dictate that rain forests be sacrificed for growing foods and for producing other goods that yield hard currency on the international market.

A global population that did not reach a billion people until about 1830 grew to two billion by 1930, and has exploded upward ever since. Much of this growth has occurred in the tropics, as diseases have been brought under control and people have, at least in certain regions, gained better access to food and clean drinking water.

The total world population in 1950 stood at about 2.5 billion people; in early 1990 it passed 5.3 billion. More than 95 million people, a number larger than the population of Mexico or that of any country in Europe except for the Soviet Union, are added to (Continued on page 30)

Shy and futile gesture of a Yanomami child in Brazil fleetingly blocks intrusion into his vulnerable world. Habitat destruction and recently introduced diseases plague many indigenous groups.

Burned forest in Brazil converts to pastureland even as it smolders. Fragile soils soon become depleted, requiring more clearing. Scientists see long-term effects from the release of carbon dioxide from burning trees.

the world population every year. These people must be fed, clothed, and assimilated into their economic and social systems. The 4.1 billion people who live in developing countries have only about 16 percent of the world's wealth. To make matters worse, there is a net flow of money *from* poor countries to rich ones, rather than in the other direction.

To relieve the pressure of too many hungry people in the cities, governments encourage citizens to migrate to remote rain forest territories. After felling the trees on their small tracts, these settlers raise cattle or crops. Later, when the soil is unable to support them, the people move on to clear another section of the forest. In the past such slash-and-burn agriculture was highly successful and caused no permanent loss of forest. After the people had left, mature trees were close enough to reseed the cleared areas, and seedlings would spring up and grow quickly in the sunlit gaps. This process mimicked reforestation that occurs in rain forests

when older trees fall. But today hundreds of millions of people obtain fuelwood by felling trees, and they grow food by clearing patches of tropical forest for crops.

The rain forest cannot heal its wounds. The resulting tragedy is that the forest is inexorably being used up. And if it should disappear, the people themselves would have nowhere else to turn.

Although warnings about the loss of tropical forests have been heard for decades, the 1980s saw a great increase in their urgency. The tragic extinction of so many species and the intensification of the greenhouse effect have led to a heightened interest in the fate of tropical forests.

Reforestation is one means of countering the greenhouse effect, and it could provide sustainable resources for tropical countries and their people. Replanted forests would also provide homes for some species of animals, plants, and

microorganisms that could adapt to them.

Efforts to save the rain forests call for a new internationalism, a realization that people everywhere share a role in the fate of the earth. Ways to alleviate poverty and hunger throughout the world must be found. New agreements between nations will need to be developed.

International funding could help establish parks and other protected areas where species endemic to rain forests could survive. Then, someday, if and when the human family reaches an equilibrium, those organisms would be available to repopulate the earth outside the protected areas. A few selected species could be preserved in zoos and botanical gardens, in seed banks, and in culture centers for microorganisms. We must make our choices wisely and implement them rapidly.

The remaining chapters of this book will address the amazing complexity and beauty of the plants and animals of the tropical rain forests, reveal the forests' rich bounty of useful products, discuss man's impact on the forests, and explore ways we might save them.

What we do over the next few years will have a profound effect on the way the world appears in the future. If we do not stop destroying our tropical forests, there will be little left. Now is the time to learn all we can about life in rain forests. What we discover may well help shape the quality of life on our planet. Clearly, today's opportunities will not come again. We live in a time when action is essential—to save as many as possible of the multitudes of plants and animals that not only inhabit the rain forest but also, in the truest sense, *are* the rain forest.

Forest untouched and forest torched, both in Brazil, present dramatic choices. Left in their natural state, rain forests renew themselves perpetually. If clear-cut, the bare earth bakes dry, only to be eroded by driving rains. If the land is replanted, the resulting forest lacks the diversity of the original.

EYELASH VIPER WITH ANOLE ON HELICONIA

Mosaic

"The rain forest has been described as a place where almost anything can live and almost everything does."

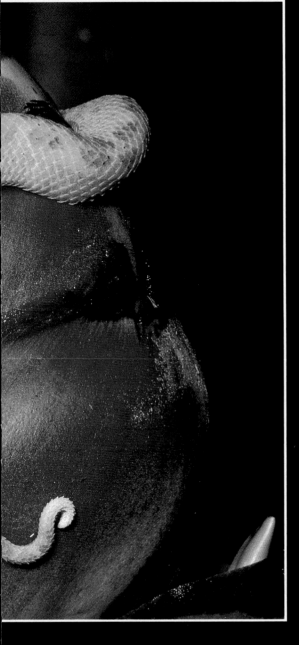

by
Cynthia Russ Ramsay

# of Life

Nothing moved. The landscape, so full of trees and entwined with vegetation, seemed strangely empty of wildlife. The metallic whine of cicadas merely underscored the vast, brooding silence. From time to time, a staccato birdsong sounded above the monotonous chorus. It was an eerie, primordial stillness, heavy with humidity and shadowed by luxuriant growth that transformed midmorning into a green twilight. I could easily imagine I had stepped into a forest from earth's distant past.

Somewhere high above, gibbons and monkeys crouched unseen in the treetops. In the same mighty trees lurked giant flying squirrels the size of house cats, snakes, lying in wait for prey. On the soggy ground clouded leopards, wild pigs, and deer had left their tracks. Large droppings marked the passage of a herd of elephants. But on that sultry day I saw none of these shy creatures that inhabit the tropical rain forests of Borneo, the largest island in the Malay archipelago.

Yet the trees, as tall as 20-story buildings, impressed me with their majesty, and my awe acquired a deeper dimension as I became more acquainted with the rain forest—the most diverse, the most complex, and the least understood ecosystem on earth.

During my travels in Southeast Asia, to preserves on the Malay Peninsula, on Borneo, and in Thailand, I sought out scientists working against time to understand the rain forest. In spite of great progress, its every corner still holds secrets waiting to be uncovered. Entomologists, for example, can still go out with a net and in five minutes turn up an insect not yet known to science. Some rain forest species are so rare, and their densities so low, that scientists know them only from a single encounter. Trees identified 50 to 100 years ago in Amazonia have not been seen since. Animals are so well hidden by the foliage that sightings are few. I, for example, was rarely able to see the birds whose songs rang through the forest.

"It's quite easy to walk past an orangutan and never know it is just overhead, sitting in a tree. A boar might be a few feet from us, but it can slip away quietly despite its size. Even elephants are hard to find during the day," a young ecologist told me after we had waited in vain in the wilderness of Borneo's Danum Valley for the appearance of wildlife.

Rain forest animals are notoriously elusive, many of them resting motionless amid the lush foliage for most of the day. One scientist stalked Sumatran rhino for so many months that he was able to identify the footprints of individual animals —but he never spotted a single one of the beasts. Nor is it easy to find tigers. A naturalist I met has heard them growl and mew. He has been close enough to detect their strong, musty onion smell. But after working 20 years in the forests of the Malay Peninsula, he has never seen one. Even the hornbills, large birds with long beaks and powerful wings, are exceptionally wary. To observe their feeding habits, one ecologist built a 40-foot blind next to a fruiting tree, working at night so the birds would not associate the blind with human intruders. In the morning the creatures flapped by in a noisy whir of wings, saw a change in their surroundings, and never returned.

Insects, which populate the rain forest in unimaginable numbers, also tend to stay out of sight—spending their lives in the ground litter, high up in the canopy, inside plant stems, or under tree bark. Some species are concealed by camouflage. A katydid that looks like a leaf, a caterpillar that blends in with the debris on the forest floor, a stick insect in the shape of a twig—these virtually defy detection.

Yet not every creature keeps a low profile. For some it pays to advertise. The tiny dart-poison frogs of the New World tropics, or Neotropics, proclaim their presence with vivid jewel hues and striking patterns. Such conspicuous good looks may help predators recognize the frogs as inedible. Many butterflies flaunt beautiful colors not only to lure potential mates but also to remind birds that they make a bad-tasting meal. Other butterfly species mimic these bold warning colorations—like sheep in wolves' clothing—and fool enemies into staying away.

I could usually count on seeing butterflies fluttering (Continued on page 38)

Splashy **Calosta cinnabarina** *puffballs* *depend on raindrops to launch clouds* *of spores. Such interdependencies* *knit rain forest species into* *intricate and delicate ecosystems.*

Hermit hummingbird's racing metabolism demands hundreds of nectar stops daily. The passionflower depends on the bird to collect and disperse its pollen. As the hummer goes from blossom to blossom, its head brushes against stamens and pistils, pollinating the flowers.

in gaudy clusters on the riverbanks, their rainbow colors glittering like miniature mosaics against the foliage. Sometimes I caught glimpses of animals at dawn and dusk, when numerous species move about and feed. At night, in blackness charged with chirping katydids and choruses of lovesick frogs calling for mates, the beam of a headlamp might reveal the glowing eyes of a civet cat or those of a diminutive mouse deer only eight inches tall.

An astounding diversity of wildlife flourishes in the rain forests of the world. A National Academy of Science report estimates that four square miles typically contain 125 species of mammals, 400 species of birds, and 100 species of reptiles. Two sites in Ecuador have yielded 74 species of frogs and toads within 1.2 square miles of forest. One study found that a single tree in Amazonian Peru accommodated 43 species of ants, about the same number as in all of Canada. The forests of the Federation of Malaysia (which includes the Malay Peninsula and the Bornean states of Sabah and Sarawak) harbor 111 species of terrestrial snakes, 80 species of lizards, and 1,000 species of butterflies —probably more per acre than any other place on earth.

This biological richness begins with the enormous array of plant life. For the great 19th-century British naturalist Alfred Russel Wallace, the thousands of plant forms complicated his research along the Amazon and in the East Indies. Writing in *Tropical Nature and Other Essays,* he complained, "If the traveller notices a particular species and wishes to find more like it, he may often turn his eyes in vain in every direction. Trees of varied forms, dimensions and colours are all around him, but he rarely sees any of them repeated. Time after time he goes to a tree which looks like the one he seeks, but a closer examination proves it to be distinct. He may at length, perhaps, meet with a second speci-

men a half mile off, or he may fail altogether, till on another occasion he stumbles on one by accident."

This great diversity, however, is music to the ears of Harvard ecologist Dr. Mark Leighton, who spends six months each year directing research in Indonesia's Gunung Palung Nature Reserve in Kalimantan, the southern two-thirds of Borneo.

"The rain forests of Southeast Asia are among the oldest ecosystems on earth. Here you can see the full flowering of evolution. Life-forms have been a hundred million years in the making, flourishing without interruption by the Ice Age climate and glaciers that extinguished so many species in temperate forests," Mark told me as we traveled upriver to the remote research camp in the reserve. The two-day boat trip in the vast delta of the Kapuas River took us past stilt-root mangrove swamps and walls of feathery nipa palm and pandanus. On the evening of the second day we entered a stream so narrow that trees enclosed our route and so shallow that our two boatmen spent much of the next six hours lugging the canoelike sampan over sandbars and logs.

"The warm climate and plentiful moisture of the rain forest provide the most favorable conditions for the processes of life and have created the greatest abundance of plant and animal species on earth—and also the most crowded. So although nature does not set harsh terms, life in the forest is highly competitive," Mark said. "Its myriad plants and animals compete and coexist by developing subtle and complex relationships and survival strategies that have brought forth a great variety of fantastic forms and life-styles."

The rain forest has been described as a place where *(Continued on page 45)*

Sunlight filters through a forest canopy in Venezuela. Habitat to millions of species of plants and animals, such canopies remain, in one scientist's words, "the last great frontier of biology."

Monkeys around the world reflect rain forest diversity. From South America, the red uakari (above) takes its nickname, "English monkey," from a perceived resemblance to gin-soaked colonials. Crimson markings help an African mandrill (left) attract mates and drive away rivals. Some macaques (right), from Southeast Asia, spend much time on the ground, but most monkeys are canopy dwellers. Costa Rican capuchins (top, right) search all forest levels for fruit, seeds, and other food.

41

Still life: Synonymous with indolence, a sloth hangs motionless for hours at a time. Sloths eat, sleep, mate, and give birth in forest canopies. On the ground they are virtually helpless. Weak hind legs and long, curved claws make walking awkward.

almost anything can live and almost everything does. Take the pink Malayan mantis, with legs lobed like petals, that masquerades as an orchid. Or moths disguised as wasps, caterpillars that look like leaves, bird-eating spiders, and ants that use their silk-producing larvae like the shuttles of a loom to bind leaves together for nests. The catalog of curiosities in Southeast Asia also includes plants that are predators, drowning and digesting insects in pitchers formed by leaf tips. And who could overlook giant rafflesia blossoms, measuring three feet across, that lure pollinating flies with an odor like that of rotting meat.

Each dawn, as the light seeped through the tracery of leaves and the gibbons awakened me with their melancholy hooting, I could anticipate a day of many surprises, for nature is at its most inventive and extravagant in the dim, damp world of the rain forest.

Oddities in the Neotropics are no less amazing. In this hothouse incubator of marvels, animals have evolved in hard-to-believe ways: six-inch-long beetles with hooks on their legs for climbing trees, frogs that backpack eggs in pouches, stingless bees that feed on carcasses, giant ants that scream before they sting, and the hard-shelled cannonball fruit that explodes its seeds into the air when it crashes to the ground. Out of the New World also come the giant anaconda, a nonvenomous snake up to 30 feet long; the paca, a 22-pound rodent that growls like a dog; and the world's smallest monkey, the pygmy marmoset that, when fully grown, is less than 5 inches tall and weighs only about 4 ounces.

Hands and feet so much alike (right) make midair snacking (left) a snap for an orangutan in Sabah's Kabili-Sepilok Forest Reserve. At a rehabilitation center here staff members teach survival skills to illegally captured young orangutans.

The region also lays claim to the shaggy, baby-faced sloth, whose fur is green with algae and inhabited by its own species of moth. This mammal leads a lethargic, upside-down existence, staying motionless for hours and even mating and giving birth while suspended from a branch. Almost as sedentary is the bristle-crested hoatzin, a two-foot-long bird that clambers awkwardly through the trees. Its young make better climbers, hauling themselves up branches by means of two large claws on each wing.

In contrast to these clumsy arboreal eccentrics the spider monkeys are restless, agile creatures, leaping through the trees like trapeze artists. For their aerobatics these monkeys have an "extra hand"—a prehensile tail with a pad of nonskid skin at the tip. This fifth limb, which can be wrapped around a branch, can gather food, brush away insects, hold an infant. Only New World monkeys have developed prehensile tails, despite their usefulness in canopy living.

The aerialists of Southeast Asia are the gibbons, which have no tails at all. These small, gray-furred apes swing from branch to branch, from tree to tree,

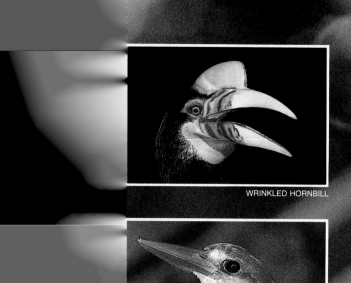

WRINKLED HORNBILL

RESPLENDENT QUETZAL

RUFOUS-BACKED KINGFISHER

KING VULTURE

KEEL-BILLED TOUCAN

BLACK-NECKED RED COTINGA

Some 2,600 bird species, three in ten on earth, live only in the rain forest. A fifth of all known species—including the black-necked red cotinga—inhabit the Amazon. Shrinking but richly varied tracts in Central America harbor the resplendent quetzal, treasured by ancient Aztec and Maya.

The king vulture is the Americas' most colorful scavenger. In New World or Old oddities flourish: Borneo's kingfisher nests only in anthills; the hornbill's head sports a bony casque. Like the hornbill, the toucan uses its outsize beak to eat large fruits; both play major roles as seed dispersers.

moving arm over arm in a form of locomotion called brachiation. Sometimes they let go and leap distances of up to 30 feet.

I heard them crashing through the tangle of foliage and vines before I saw them—shadows with long arms flitting 40 feet above the forest floor. I was surprised at how fast they moved.

"They're tremendously nimble, but apparently they have their share of accidents," said Dr. Warren Y. Brockelman, the American director of Mahidol University's Center for Conservation Biology in Bangkok, Thailand. "An examination of wild gibbon skeletons revealed that at least half had evidence of fractures."

We had come to Warren's gibbon study site in Khao Yai National Park, north of Bangkok, where he has been following one family of gibbons—a mated pair and their offspring—for ten years. Normally gibbons flee through the upper canopy if anyone approaches, but these apes had become habituated to human observers and tolerated our presence. Using binoculars and craning our necks, we had a good view of them foraging for fruit about 60 feet up in the canopy. The female did not appear to be hampered by the dark, spindly infant clinging to her as she vaulted through the trees. Young gibbons don't gain much weight until about two years of age, when they no longer rely on their mothers for transportation.

No other apes are so strongly territorial. After their early morning songs to warn off any possible gibbon trespassers —performances that can last as long as two hours—the family spends the day roaming its turf, searching for food. Gibbons prefer fruit, consuming some 100 varieties that ripen at various times of year; but they also eat shoots, insects, nestling birds, and eggs. By four o'clock the gibbons are fast asleep, sitting with knees up against their chests and their heads on their knees.

"These animals need a lot of rest, because they can't swing around in the trees safely if they're tired or less than fully alert," said Warren, as we scrambled to keep up with the family.

Thrashing through the forest gave me a quick and painful introduction to rattans, the climbing palms of Southeast Asia's rain forests. These palms produce slender leaf tips three to six feet long, like whips studded with recurved spines that enable the rattans to latch onto nearby vegetation. They grapple their way up into the sunlight of the canopy, snag by snag. The barbs also pierce clothing and skin. I learned that pulling away only digs the spines in deeper. It takes a while to free yourself from one of these tendrils— one hook at a time, earning the rattan the name "the wait-a-minute plant."

On any trip into the tropical rain forest the going may be tough, but for me the journey was not the "green hell" I had feared. Granted, malaria was always a dread possibility, because new strains resistant to chloroquine and other prophylactics are constantly appearing. And there are also the hazards of scrub typhus, leptospirosis, assorted fevers, and hundreds of species of parasitic worms.

From time to time I may have felt the menace of the rain forest, but the power and magic of that marvelously primeval place have left a stronger mark on my memory. Like the night I came upon luminescent fungi glimmering in the darkness with a pale green light. Another night was filled with the sound of rain that had ended earlier in the evening, but leaves with drip-tips prolonged the shower for hours more. One dawn with mist seeping across the landscape, I awoke to the soft-eyed stare of a red leaf monkey watching me from its leafy perch. Nor will I forget the sight of an army of termites on the march, like a rippling ribbon on the forest floor, guarded at regular intervals by soldiers of the species.

Fortunately, the places I visited were remarkably free of flies, mosquitoes, mites, and gnats, which torment life in some rain forests, particularly in the seasonally flooded parts of the Amazon basin.

The 19th-century German naturalist Alexander von Humboldt, on a journey up Venezuela's Orinoco River, tried burying himself in sand and applying rancid crocodile grease in a futile effort to escape the pests. Despite the advent of repellents, travelers may be plagued by clouds of insects or by such nasty tropical pests as the botfly maggot, which burrows under the skin, embeds itself with hooks, and remains until it emerges weeks later as an inch-long larva.

Although there are king cobras, kraits, and pit vipers in the places I went, danger from them has been exaggerated. I saw only one snake during my weeks in Southeast Asia. Apparently, though, encounters with snakes may be as much as five or ten times more frequent in African and Amazonian rain forests. In Southeast Asia the trees are more dangerous than the snakes. As Mark Leighton tells newcomers to his camp, the probability of snakebite is lower than the risk of injury from a clunk on the head by a falling branch.

Trees are also trellises for lianas, woody climbing plants of many species. These climbers enjoy an advantage. They don't need to build their own support and can expend all their energy escaping the darkness of the forest floor. Once in the canopy, many lianas branch out and form a dense network that can hold a tree upright even after its trunk has been severed by a chain saw. Some vines dangle like great twisting ropes that might carry a Tarzan. Sometimes the lianas spiral up again, twining around a second and third tree in giant webs.

Strangler figs also need trees for support. Each starts up high, germinating from a seed deposited by a bird or a mammal in a fork or hollow. From this toehold the fig grows downward, sending aerial roots into the soil, roots that gradually encase the trunk of the host tree. As the roots capture the moisture and minerals in the soil, the seedling fig grows rapidly skyward, cutting off the sunlight with its leafy boughs. Eventually, the host tree—starved of moisture, nutrients, and sunlight—dies.

The first time I saw one of these killers, the imprisoned tree had rotted away, and only the giant fig remained, rising from its latticework of roots around a hollow core.

Equally striking was the profusion of plants growing on plants. Sometimes it seemed that every available surface was buried beneath orchids, ferns, mosses, and other epiphytic plants. As many as 30 species of epiphytes may carpet a single tree. Their high-rise habitat gives many of these "air plants" a head start in the competition for sunlight but denies them access to the moisture and nutrients stored in the soil. Epiphytes have made remarkable adaptations to meet their needs, for they are not parasites, which pirate their means of subsistence. Many epiphytic orchids either hoard rainwater in bulbous stems or use free-hanging roots covered with a whitish tissue to soak up moisture from the humid air. Nourishment comes from the minerals and minute particles of organic matter carried in rainwater and collected in the cracks of bark.

Most rain forest orchids are small and difficult to see in the canopy. Although there are about 3,000 orchid species in Borneo, the epiphytic ferns were far more conspicuous, and I soon came to recognize those with long, upright leaves that create their own soil. Malaysian botanist Dr. Francis Ng calls them litter-trapping plants.

"For example, the bird's-nest fern, growing on a tree, takes a basket shape that catches debris drifting down from the branches above. As the litter accumulates, it decomposes into humus soon colonized by lichens, fungi, insects, and a host of microscopic organisms," said Dr. Ng, a scientist who has explored the natural world of the Malay Peninsula for many years.

"The ferns then grow roots that take nourishment from their self-contained

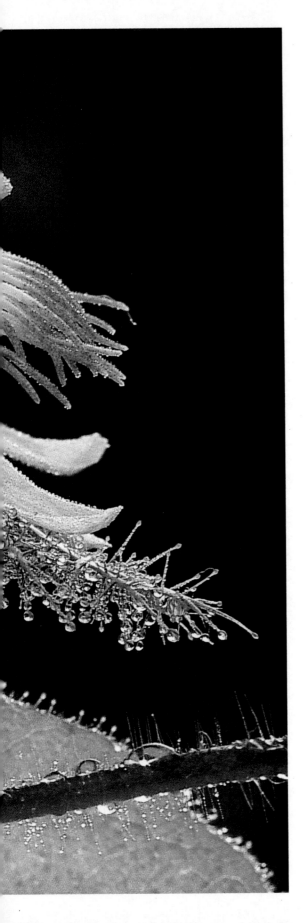

hanging gardens," Dr. Ng explained, as we talked at the Forest Research Institute Malaysia in the suburbs of Kuala Lumpur. "Some trees rid themselves of epiphytes by periodically shedding their bark; others may deter these hangers-on with bark that is poisonous or too smooth to provide an anchor hold for seeds."

Epiphytes do not directly harm their hosts, but clearly I had entered a battle-field where multitudes of plants were waging a perpetual war for a little more sun, a little more nourishment.

Although the landscape remains densely green, most of the trees of Asian rain forests lose all their leaves for a short time—quickly replacing them with a new set in a few days or weeks. The tallest of all the rain forest plants is one of these "briefly deciduous" trees. Topping out at more than 250 feet, *Koompassia excelsa* produces branches with a smooth, pale bark. When the tree sheds its leaves, its bare limbs add a strange skeletal accent to the verdant richness. One day in Sabah's Danum Valley, when the sky was a dark canvas for white, billowing clouds, I marveled at the bare twiggy boughs of this species flaring above the dense canopy like a filigree parasol. Not far away, another tree of the same species, responding to its own timetable, retained its leafy crown.

Many rain forest trees replace their leaves in flushes of new growth. At first I mistook the young leaves for flowers, for many of them were red and dangled limply from the branches, like tassels.

"The color comes from chemicals called anthocyanins, which are believed to mop up ultraviolet radiation and protect the young leaves from the strong sunlight of the tropics," said Nicholas Brown, a doctoral candidate from Oxford University's Forestry Institute in England. Nick had

Passiflora foetida *and about 450 other passionflower species take their name from the passion of Christ. Spanish priests saw a crown of thorns in the decorative fringe typical of these flowers.*

EPIDENDRUM

"They reveal the imagination of God"— a scientist marvels at rain forest flowers.

BOMAREA MULTIFLORA

ROUND-HEAD GINGER

Flowers of the rain forest surprise and delight the careful observer: from the flashy yellow and red bracts of the Heliconia and the eerie human face in an Epidendrum *orchid to the delicate round-head ginger, the brilliant* Bomarea multiflora, *and the bromeliad called cup-of-flame.*

CUP-OF-FLAME BROMELIAD

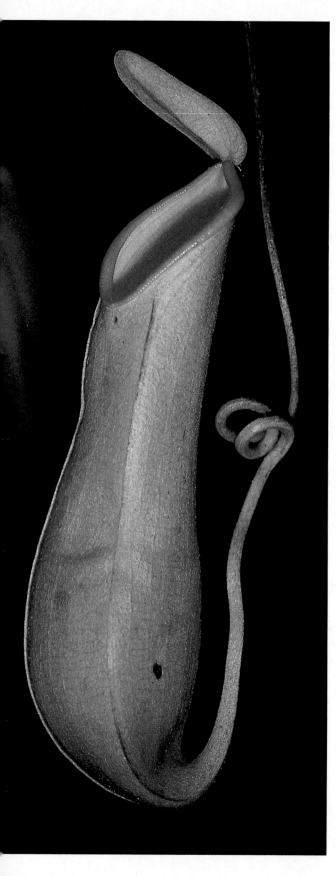

come to the Danum Valley Field Centre, a research and educational facility run by the Sabah Foundation. For the past two years he had been working on a project with Donald Kennedy of the University of Aberdeen in Scotland to study regeneration in the gaps left by tree falls.

At first it was hard for me to believe how frequently trees and boughs come crashing down, even though I heard the loud crack of falling branches every day. On one occasion, I was startled by a tremendous explosion. We found a toppled giant less than half a mile away, swathed in a chaotic mass of lianas that had been wrenched to the ground along with a couple of small trees. No storm, not even a whisper of wind, had provoked the fall.

"Sometimes the big trees become too soggy and top-heavy after a rain and just lose their balance," Don told me.

The high rate of tree fall is not surprising, for the roots have a rather feeble grip on the ground, lying, for the most part, in the top one or two inches of soil.

On the trails of the Danum Valley Conservation Area, I could plainly see that the canopy was not really a continuous, unbroken layer, for here and there fragments of light dappled the pervading shade. I was also surprised by the density of seedlings and saplings cluttering the lower levels of the rain forest.

"All those stunted trees are just sitting tight, waiting for a chance in the sun," said Don. "Most of them will remain suppressed in the understory and never reach maturity."

Opportunity had arrived for the plants in one of the larger canopy gaps, which Nick and Don had created to monitor growth rates by measuring leaf sizes and seedling heights at regular intervals.

Function has shaped the pitcher plant leaf into a deadly snare. Fragrance lures insects and, rarely, frogs or mice to the pitcher's slippery lip. Victims fall in and drown in digestive liquids (opposite, in cross section).

"Ultimately only one or two trees will reach the canopy here. In a temperate forest, where a few species always compete with the same rivals, betting on the outcome isn't exactly exciting. But in a rain forest the vast numbers of species, or players, make it almost impossible to predict which of these trees will win this round of competition," said Nick.

Many of these young trees-in-waiting were dipterocarps, towering giants when they mature, which dominate Southeast Asia's rain forests and may account for half the trees in the canopy. Some species grow to be 200 to 250 feet tall, soaring 75 feet or more before their first branches appear. Many dipterocarps have large flattened buttresses flaring from the base of the trunks. These projections are distinctive features of the landscape; and, like the web of hanging plants, they contribute to the magnificence of the forest. Most scientists now believe buttresses, some of them as much as 30 feet in height, are like guy ropes on a tent, bracing trees weakly anchored by shallow roots that often sprawl across the ground like undulating snakes.

Because the humus layer is thin, and the topsoil in many rain forests has been leached by millions of years of heavy rains, most roots grow horizontally along the surface, where they absorb nutrients concentrated in the litter on the forest floor. The operation is so efficient that trees are able to achieve great stature despite the depleted soil. Some of the finest stands thrive on the poorest land.

In the rain forest, litter can decompose in six weeks, 60 times faster than in northern conifer forests. Termites are important among the agents of decay, chewing up dead wood like mechanical mulchers and digesting the cellulose with the help of protozoans or bacteria in their gut. Other bacteria and fungi also play a vital role in decomposition, doing the job chemically by secreting enzymes that break down plant tissue. The minute fungal filaments that penetrate the detritus were hard to see, but their fruit-bodies, emerging from the drab litter in graceful umbrella, petal, or fan shapes, added stabs of orange, yellow, or white to the brown monochrome of the forest floor.

As I walked along, I often heard the sharp, singsong call of the Indian cuckoo reverberating over and over through the forest. It was one of the most familiar sounds of my journey. The cadence of its three phrases has earned it the name "Beethoven's Fifth" bird.

As obvious as the concert was the scarcity of flowers. "Blame it on the dipterocarps. It may take 60 years before a tree matures and produces blossoms for the first time. After that it flowers at irregular intervals, once every three, five, or seven years, without a consistent pattern or cycle. You could spend several years here and never see it in bloom," Nick told me.

Eventually a climatic trigger, which may be a cold snap or a dry spell, sets off a phenomenon called gregarious or synchronous flowering. When this occurs, nearly all dipterocarp species bloom within a period of several weeks. The trees have yet another timing trick; the species all produce fruit at the same time. Nick explained why this is an effective strategy.

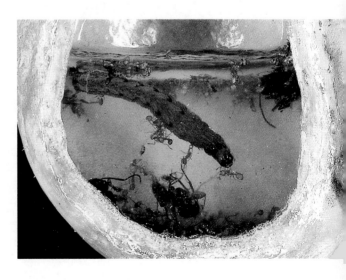

"If a species were to fruit separately, it would become a honeypot, with all the seed-eaters from miles around flocking in to feed," he said. "Chances are the whole crop would be wiped out. But massive, sporadic fruiting by many species saturates the market, so there's a greater likelihood some seeds will survive."

To produce seeds most rain forest trees rely on animals for pollination instead of wind.

"Species are too widely dispersed to depend on random breezes," said Dr. Yap Son Kheong, a botanist helping to take an inventory of the vegetation in the Rompin Forest Reserve, an area in Peninsular Malaysia being targeted as part of a new national park. I tagged along as Dr. Yap set out from base camp on the Kinchin River to collect flowers.

"Except for the trees that are apomictic—can develop fruit without fertilization—there's a lot of competition among plants for animals to disperse pollen," said Dr. Yap. "Some species can coexist because their flowering times are staggered and they can share pollinators. This also guarantees a steady supply of food for the pollinators all through the year. Other plants have evolved highly specialized features and life-styles that attract specific animals," said Dr. Yap, introducing me to the fascinating subject of pollination ecology.

Shreds of cottony mist drifted down from the forested ridges as we left the riverbank and entered the narrow corridors of the forest, where a canopy of interlocking branches reduced vistas to small patches of sky. Had it not been for a scattering of tiny, pale yellow petals strewn on the ground like confetti, I would never have known a tree was in bloom—so small were the blossoms, so distant the boughs.

Of all the plants none are more ingenious in attracting pollinators than the rain forest orchids. One species entices male wasps with flowers that look like the

female wasp. Other orchids mimic aphids, caterpillars, fungi, or flies, with the result that they lure their predators. In South America many epiphytic orchids provide male Euglossine bees with perfume they need for their courtship ritual. As long as these iridescent bees are in the neighborhood, they also pollinate Brazil nut trees. A business venture to raise Brazil nuts on a plantation failed to take this natural balance into account. Without orchids there were no bees. Without bees the flowers of the Brazil nut trees remained sterile—and as a result there were no nuts.

Figs and wasps have also perfected an extraordinary one-on-one relationship. "It's a process of mutual coevolution," said Dr. Yap, who then explained that each fig species (and there are about a thousand) is pollinated by its own special wasp that must have the fig flower as a place to lay her eggs. The alchemy of coevolution has so entwined the figs and wasps that without each other neither could reproduce.

Forest interactions complex and bizarre: Sprouting antennalike, the spore-laden stalk of a Cordyceps *fungus (left) signals doom for a Costa Rican weevil as the fungus slowly digests it from the inside out; in Cameroon ants colonize the hollow stems of the* Barteria *tree (cutaway, above) and in exchange for shelter seem to protect the tree by attacking its insect enemies.*

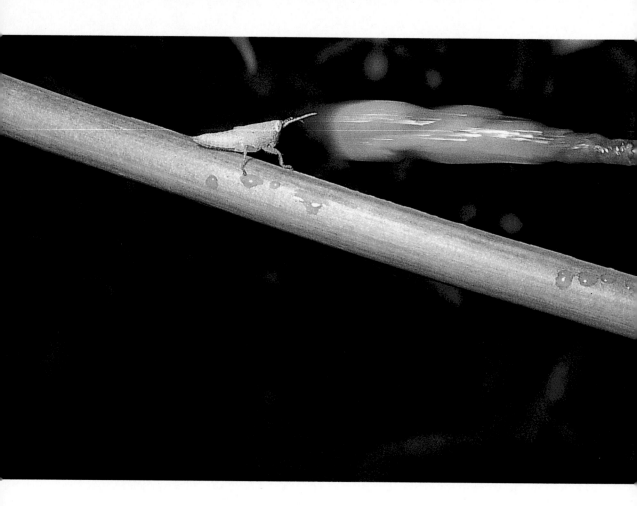

I had heard about trees, like the cacao, sprouting flowers and fruits directly from the trunk and larger branches, but it still was astonishing to see blossoms ornamenting bark like corsages. This primarily rain forest phenomenon, called cauliflory, caters to specific pollinators like bats, which need open space to maneuver and roost while sipping nectar. Cauliflory is also a tactic for dispersing seeds, capitalizing on those fruit-eating animals that avoid the crowded canopy to feed.

At a shrubby Macaranga tree I discovered another kind of alliance between animals and plants. The hollow stems at the bases of leaves were riddled with colonies of ants nesting and breeding. In exchange for the hospitality the ants protected the plant from leaf-eating insects, such as caterpillars, and picked off potentially damaging eggs and larvae.

"Apparently some of the trees are so dependent on these lodgers that they re-ward them by producing starch granules the ants like to eat," Dr. Yap explained.

In general the leaves of tropical vines and trees are efficient producers of various chemicals. "Easily double the number in temperate-zone plants," says American entomologist Dr. Daniel Janzen, who is studying plant–animal interactions in Costa Rica. "Many of these chemicals are highly toxic and defend plants against the heavy traffic of insects and other foragers in the tropics, where there is no winter to knock back the population of herbivores."

In another partnership bullhorn acacias rely on ants to attack damaging insects and to cut off encroaching vines that might cast too much shade. Experiments by Janzen indicate that without their ants the acacias suffer severe damage and in most locations would be "reduced to the point of extinction."

The diversity and interdependence of plants and animals in the rain forest enthralls Janzen, who in measuring the complexity of human achievement against the complexities of the rain forest states that it's like comparing a mouse's squeak to music.

Nature's ingenuity is not always benign. There is nothing quite like the devastation wrought by the hordes of *Eciton* ants of Amazonia and the blind driver ants of Africa, which march in columns of millions, consuming all small creatures in their path. "Wherever they move, the whole animal world is set in commotion, and every creature tries to get out of their way," wrote 19th-century naturalist Henry Walter Bates, who spent ten years along the Amazon.

Recent studies reveal that even these scourges of the forest bolster the well-being of some wildlife. Biologists Adrian Forsyth and Ken Miyata in their book *Tropical Nature* describe the bird and insect camp followers that take advantage of the flushing effect of the ant raids. Neotropical antbirds depend on the raiding columns. As the grasshoppers, moths, katydids, and other insects jump or fly to escape the ants, the birds swoop down, chattering and peeping as they gorge themselves. Joining the hangers-on are the translucent-winged ithomiid butterflies, which hover in the vicinity and feed on the nitrogen-rich droppings of the antbirds.

Entomologists consider the rain forest a paradise for studying ants, but I was less than delighted with my close encounter with them. One night in Borneo fire

In a split second a chameleon seizes a grasshopper dinner. This mechanical marvel of a tongue, longer than the lizard's body, lies folded in the back of the mouth until muscle action shoots it out; a hollow bulblike tip captures prey.

These night creatures face a dim future despite elusive ways. The armor-plated pangolin, a toothless mammal native to Africa, may ward off some predators—but not humans who sell its scales for home remedies. Ring-tailed lemurs (below) cling to existence in their dwindling habitat in Madagascar. The aye-aye (left), a primate of Madagascar, has a long middle finger that can scoop insect larvae from under tree bark.

ants swarmed through my quarters in tens of thousands, carpeting the raised platform where I slept beneath a mosquito net. The chaotic army, moving in all directions, blanketed my duffel bag and buried my sandals, but I was safe from their painful stings as long as I nabbed the strays that penetrated the netting. I kept vigil with my flashlight until just before dawn, when all at once the ants were gone.

Any short stroll in the rain forest put me in touch with the blood-sucking ground leech, another unpleasant inhabitant of Southeast Asian rain forests. It was some consolation to know the wormlike creatures carry no diseases. As one scientist put it, perhaps that is part of their deal with God, for no animal preys on them.

I wore tightly woven knee-length "leech stockings" over trousers tucked into regular socks. Usually this was adequate protection against the leeches that hunched up my legs, searching for a place to sink their jaws, which have three sharp teeth. When bloated with blood, the leeches simply dropped off; otherwise they were firmly attached by suction pads at both ends. I loathed tugging on the rubbery creatures, for they would roll onto my hands, hanging on in the spaces between my fingers. I finally learned that a leech has less traction when it draws itself together as it loops along; then I could simply flick it away.

Creatures more charming drew me to the Kabili-Sepilok Forest Reserve, a refuge for orangutans, whose numbers are steadily shrinking because of the destruction of their habitat. Here the government

of Sabah runs a rehabilitation center for orangutans that have been injured or illegally captured, usually by loggers. Without their mothers, these orphans had not learned to forage for food, build nests, or even climb trees. While these orange-haired juveniles learn the ways of the wild, staff members set out fruits and milk for

them on small platforms and encourage them to climb among low branches.

At these feeding stations visitors from all over the world watch the antics of the unfettered young apes with their expressive faces. Among the first things that caught my attention were their dexterous feet, which serve as a second pair of hands.

Orangs grasp objects with either hands or feet, and I saw them peeling bananas with their lips, which they twist and purse into spoon shapes. One juvenile seemed to prefer somersaults to walking. Another repeatedly placed a bucket over its head and then frantically removed it; a younger orang sat nearby with studied indifference, slyly glancing in the direction of the game, but lunged for the toy as soon as it had been abandoned.

Long-term studies of orangutans, which are found only in Borneo and Sumatra, have begun to yield some insights into this species—the least understood and the most solitary of the great apes. Primatologist Biruté Galdikas has spent thousands of hours since 1971 observing orangutans in the wild. She believes orangutans—the largest bodied fruit-eaters on earth—just can't risk being too gregarious. In forests where so many trees fruit sporadically and where favorite foods, like figs, are so widely scattered, a solitary life-style reduces competition for food. If a group of orangs tried to harvest a fruiting tree, says Dr. Galdikas, it would be stripped before all had enough to eat.

Figs may be the single most important source of food for fruit-eating animals in the Neotropics and in Southeast Asia. One species of fig or other is always in fruit. "The bustling activity at a large fig is one of the unforgettable spectacles of the forest," notes John Terborgh, an American ecologist working in the Cocha Cashu forest of Peru's Manu National Park. Observing the varieties of monkeys and birds feeding simultaneously, Terborgh has wondered what mysterious perception guides them to that spot. He speculates that the animals are summoned by the shrill din of a myriad of parakeets.

It's not easy finding a fruiting tree in the rain forest, and the hornbills of Southeast Asia must fly great distances for their favored food. These large birds with a bizarre, bony protuberance on their bills

All that glitters in an inky pool may be Costa Rican male golden toads. Nearly voiceless, they lure mates by luster. Amplexus takes place (at top) as male clasps female: Eggs are deposited and sperm unite with them in the water.

and lashes on their eyelids rove territories that cover several square miles. Like the toucans of the Neotropics, hornbills have huge bills adapted for feeding on fruit.

"Hornbills learn where their food trees are and make a beeline for them," Mark Leighton told me on a stroll along the trails of the Cabang Panti Research Station in Kalimantan. "More than 50 species of trees depend exclusively on these birds to disperse their seeds. By staggering the sequence of fruiting to reduce competition, a whole assortment of plants has acquired the birds as regular customers. The

purpose, of course, is propagation. After feeding, the birds carry the seeds away from the shadow of the parent trees to places where they may have enough sunlight and space to grow. It's another example of the coevolution of animals and plants, a process that has helped create the diversity of the rain forest."

One morning I was lucky to see bushy-crested hornbills feeding in a mammoth fig tree. They would dive down to pluck a fruit, promptly take off, and in minutes repeat the operation, filling the air with the whoosh *(Continued on page 70)*

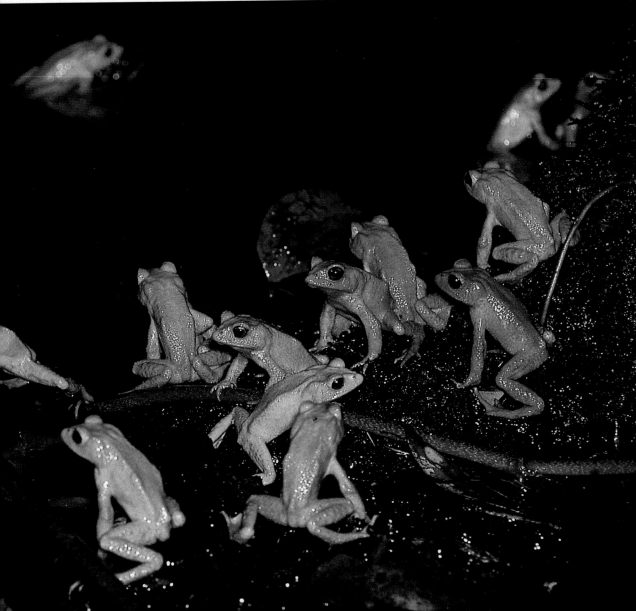

Jellied orbs enclose rain frog embryos of a species that lives mainly on the ground. These frogs skip the tadpole stage, emerging fully developed. Though reproductive methods of the earth's frogs and toads vary, many species share an unexplained decrease in number.

Tropics afford conditions for year-round breeding and growing, compressing life cycles, speeding evolution, and fostering amazing diversity among butterflies.

MORPHO BUTTERFLY

PASSION VINE BUTTERFLY

DRYAS IULIA

BURMESE JEZEBELS

GLASSWING BUTTERFLY

of their broad wings—a sound which has been likened to a locomotive going uphill.

But it is in their nesting habits that these large-billed birds are most remarkable. With the help of her mate, the female hornbill seals herself with mud and droppings inside a hollow tree, where she hatches her eggs and raises her young. The only opening is a narrow slit through which her mate delivers food. This self-imprisonment protects the eggs and chicks from the large tree-dwelling snakes and monkeys that prey on them, for voracious nest predators are one of the great hazards rain forest birds must face.

Other species of birds cope with the peril of nest predators by using spiny rattans as building material or by placing their nests at the inaccessible ends of lateral branches or on the tops of saplings away from the main thoroughfares in the canopy. The nests of some are so well hidden that, to this day, they have frustrated efforts to find them.

In the rain forest the various bird species do not have one distinct breeding season, and the parents continue to feed their young for months, even after they have left the nest.

Ornithologist Dr. Geoffrey Davison at the National University of Malaysia explained why. It's all related to the stable food supply—never abundant but without the feast or famine of the temperate zones. The tropics do not have spring's explosive burgeoning of life to trigger the urge to mate and grow rapidly.

To a visitor, it's startling to see and hear mixed-species flocks of birds foraging together for food. Davison pointed out

Camouflage reflects natural selection's fine-tuning. Shape and color match a mantis to its leafy hideaway (right). False snake eyes on a Great Mormon caterpillar may cause predators to mistake it for a snake and not eat it.

that though the flocks may be large, they rarely contain more than a few birds of the same species.

"Each kind of bird is a specialist, pursuing its own kind of plant food or insect prey; each one is searching in a particular place—inside a tree hole or at the ends of branches. The birds can assemble in these large flocks, which offer many pairs of eyes for protection, because they partition the food supply and avoid competition," said Dr. Davison.

Equally impressive is the array of breeding strategies that enable 74 species of frogs and toads to coexist in only 1.2 square miles of forest in Ecuador. By lay-

ing eggs at different times of year and by depositing them in a variety of places, these animals have shown the resourcefulness that characterizes, after all, what rain forest living is all about.

Perhaps the exquisite tacca lily, a black flower set in three white sepals at its base, embodies the rain forest's allure. I was intrigued by the long lavender filaments trailing down from the petals of this beautiful but baffling flower. I inquired of a young scientist what purpose those whiskers serve. The answer spoke to all the strange and fabulous phenomena of the forest, for he replied, "They reveal the imagination of God."

GOLDEN TORTOISE BEETLE

Lacy lobes spread beneath a female dead leaf mantis's prehensile shears. Glassy sheaths cover a golden tortoise beetle. A spiny katydid's outsize jaws and serrated legs can inflict lethal wounds on enemies.

SPINY KATYDID

DEAD LEAF MANTIS

HARVESTER WITH PALM FRUIT, WEST AFRICA

Bounty of the

*"There are tens of thousands of edible species
of fruits and leaves and vegetables, as well as roots*

by
Jennifer C. Urquhart

A slight figure stepped out of the glaring sun into the shade of the veranda. Without saying a word he handed over a tray fashioned of broad, glossy leaves. At its center nestled a large chunk of honeycomb dripping with golden honey—amber sweetness from the rain forest.

Such a special gift required a proper response. The priest at the Roman Catholic mission rose from his rattan chair, went inside, and reappeared with cigarettes and a small bag of salt. Both were accepted silently, but with obvious satisfaction—as revealed by a beaming smile. For Manda André, a Baka Pygmy, obtaining that honey was more a scene from the movie *Raiders of the Lost Ark* than a quick run to

Forest

bees with smoke, all to find the treat we enjoyed on the porch at the mission at Salapoumbe, in southeastern Cameroon.

I had come to this world in equatorial West Africa, near the border between Cameroon and the Central African Republic, to see something of the bounty that over millennia the tropical forest has bestowed upon such people as the Baka and which now, more than ever, is available to the rest of the world.

Here the forest seems to stretch without end into the Congo basin. From the air the rich green appears little disturbed, interrupted only occasionally by a silt-brown river braiding a hesitant course across the flat expanse of land, or by the firm red seam of a logging road clearly certain of its destination. At regular intervals the bare branches of deciduous kapok trees crown out above the broadleaved evergreens.

The Congo River basin, which claims nearly a fifth of the world's remaining rain forest, is home to such creatures as lowland gorillas and forest elephants. In this small corner of the region the Baka Pygmies make up about 60 percent of a sparse human population. Like other hunter-gatherers in the world's tropical forests, they sometimes cultivate staple crops or trade agricultural work and forest products, such as honey, for commodities they could not otherwise obtain. But they also continue many of their old ways, reaping from the forest a rich bounty. Leaves and fruits and roots, grubs and caterpillars, dainty duiker antelopes, gorillas and the elusive elephant—all provide sustenance. For many forest dwellers wild honey is perhaps the most sought after of nature's gifts—so prized that it is often consumed immediately. On this day we were lucky. André shared. Besides, the honey earned him a good exchange: salt, a necessity, and tobacco, a luxury.

It is becoming clear that the tropical forest is not just a place apart, albeit a most astonishingly complicated, extraordinary place. It is a world, too, of commerce and trade. This world takes form in transactions as simple as our exchange for honey on the porch and as intricate as the international market in mahogany logs. During my travels in Africa I would learn of this world—how people such as the Baka depend on the forest and how we in modern society are also linked to it.

I heard the honey bird call one morning near Salapoumbe, from high in the forest's leafy canopy. Below, on the heels of a Baka named Sama Valentin, I followed a trail with Father Robert Brisson, a priest and scholar who for more than 20 years has worked with and studied this group of Pygmies. In Baka lore, he told me, the honey bird—*mbeleko*—sings a special song near a hive to lead the Baka to the prize. (In fact, the bird is a species of honey guide.)

"The world for the Baka *is* the forest," Father Brisson has said. "It is a place where they are secure . . . where each being, plant, insect, animal, bee live as a family." The affection that French-born Brisson has for these people and his respect for their culture are evident when he speaks. "The tree is not only a bit of wood that one cuts to make money. It is a living being that speaks to them."

In intimate tones other voices of the forest have spoken to the Baka and have taught them through generations how to avoid the perils of their environment and how to make use of it. They know of fruits that ripen in cycles through the year, of roots to dig, of mushrooms in a dozen varieties. They take oil from one plant to burn for light (Continued on page 81)

Wristwatches and thongs signal contact with outside influences, yet this Pygmy woman in the Central African Republic dispels darkness in the traditional way: burning gum from a local tree. Oils from tropical plants may become more widely used as sources of energy.

In the Central African Republic, a Pygmy couple savor fresh honeycomb. Tropical forests provide food, medicine, clothing, and shelter for tribal peoples.

and leaves from another to place like roof tiles over their domed huts. Toxins from the liana *Strophanthus gratus* provide an arrow poison to bring down game animals. Rotenone from roots and stems stuns fish to make catching them easier. A type of pepper repels mosquitoes.

In the deep forest it was quiet. Sama paused occasionally to tell me about individual plants, many used medicinally. At one point he walked without hesitation up a near-vertical liana—as much to show off his agility, I think, as to grab leaves from the plant above. Here and there he plucked leaves or a twig and explained their uses. "This liana," Sama said, "is good to treat wounds. You crush the root and apply it." There wasn't a plant that I pointed to for which Sama did not have a name, a use—or several uses. Ayous, a large deciduous tree valued by loggers, is good for various maladies, including those that affect the heart. "You make a mixture of cinders with oil," Sama prescribed, "and rub the chest on the side of the heart." The bark of *Terminalia superba* offers a heart stimulant of a more psychological sort. When peeled and consumed, it assures courage for the elephant hunter.

"All the Baka children know the plants," said Brisson. It is an intimacy with their environment that they have in common with many other peoples of the tropical forest. Amazonian Indians, for example, live in harmony with their forest home, as do the Penan in Borneo. These tribal people can name and make use of hundreds of species of trees and other plants as well as animals. Scientists are now paying attention to such knowledge in the hope of finding applications for it in the modern world, particularly in agriculture and medicine.

Water gushing from a liana quenches thirst in the Congo. Certain species of the hanging vines yield life-sustaining water in areas that lack streams. On a much larger scale, tropical forests regulate water supplies and help control erosion.

In the 15th century, products native to tropical forests—especially spices—enticed explorers such as Christopher Columbus and Vasco da Gama to the earth's farthest corners. But clearly Columbus was aware of other treasures, remarking upon the Caribbean vegetation in his log: "so green and so lovely...and so different from our own...many herbs and many trees which are very valuable in Spain for dyes and for medicinal spices, but I do not know them, for which I feel great sorrow." Centuries before those adventurers sailed, the Chinese and the Southeast Asians were carrying on a busy trade in commodities of the tropical realms, exchanging aromatic oils and resins, valuable woods, spices.

By the mid-19th century Europeans had developed several major tropical forest plants as crops. Large-scale production of cinchona—the "fever bark" discovered in the Andes and much in demand for treating malaria—moved to plantations in Southeast Asia. Cacao, for chocolate, also migrated from tropical America, to Africa, where two-thirds of the world's supply is produced today. Sugarcane, on the other hand, which probably originated on New Guinea, gained widespread cultivation in the New World.

Rubber, derived from various plants native to the tropics, had long been familiar. New World inhabitants had intrigued early wanderers with samples of it. In 1839 Charles Goodyear developed the vulcanization process, and eventually *Hevea brasiliensis,* the most productive of the Amazonian species, became widely cultivated on Asian plantations.

Rubber trees flourish in Africa too. In the western reaches of Cameroon I drove a road cut straight as an arrow through row upon row of rubber trees, all leaning at the same angle as if bending to a phantom wind. Cups caught the latex that flowed from parallel rows of scars in the mottled bark. At intervals along the road

Natural pharmacy, the forest at Oku, Cameroon, supplies herbs for a healer (right). In Oku, a region known for its traditional medical practitioners, Dr. Ngeng (below) has a prospering practice. Most of the world depends on traditional healing, now studied by ethnobotanists who seek information that might enlarge modern medicine's pharmacopeia.

people gathered around trucks to tip buckets of the white liquid into vats. Young boys bounced large balls formed of strands of dried latex gleaned off the plantation. These they offered for a price to passersby, haggling over a few francs. Natural rubber—a 4-billion-dollar industry worldwide—is essential for items such as aircraft tires that require greater heat tolerance than synthetic latex possesses.

And rubber is not the only large industry dependent on products of the tropical forests. Woods, rattans, and bamboos become furniture and baskets. Nine major tropical spices are valued on the international market at hundreds of millions of dollars each year. The United States alone consumes on average 37,000 tons of black pepper annually. The resins of tropical forest trees are indispensable components of varnishes and other industrial products. Gums, oils, waxes, natural sweeteners hundreds of times sweeter than cane sugar or saccharin—all these and more come from the tropical forests.

I n reality, though far from the Baka, Yanomami, or Penan, we in the rest of the world have come to depend, as they do, upon the riches of rain forests. In my own home, for example, are rattan chairs and a carved camphorwood chest. My schefflera, spreading its glossy leaves in pale winter light, would dwarf the whole house if in its tropical environment. In my kitchen are wooden bowls and spoons and shelves of spices— cinnamon, cardamom, ginger, pepper, nutmeg—not to mention coffee, chocolate, bananas, oranges, and perhaps a mango or a papaya. In the bathroom cabinet: the flavor in the mouthwash and the cough drops. And the medicines: At least a quarter of U.S. prescription drugs—totaling an estimated 8 billion dollars in value annually—are based on plant substances, many native to tropical forests.

Sometimes the bounty is not so obvious. The warbler that trills in spring in my garden—the kind that helps control insects that would ravage temperate crops— finds its winter home in the forests of Central America. The wax that coats the pages

82

of a magazine on my rosewood coffee table comes from a tropical plant.

On the way to Korup National Park, also in western Cameroon, I learned more about the gifts of the forest. As I drove mile upon mile through oil palm plantations, the luxuriant heads of palms glistened and nodded in a driving tropical rainstorm. Later, in the park, which boasts one of the richest biomes in all of Africa, I watched a machete slice effortlessly through one of the many stout lianas that loop from the forest canopy. Out of the severed vine clear water gushed, sweet, delicious as

Holding an antelope horn, Dr. Ngeng invokes the healing powers of the spirit world. His son, Joseph Nforma, applies herbals to a patient suffering from seizures.

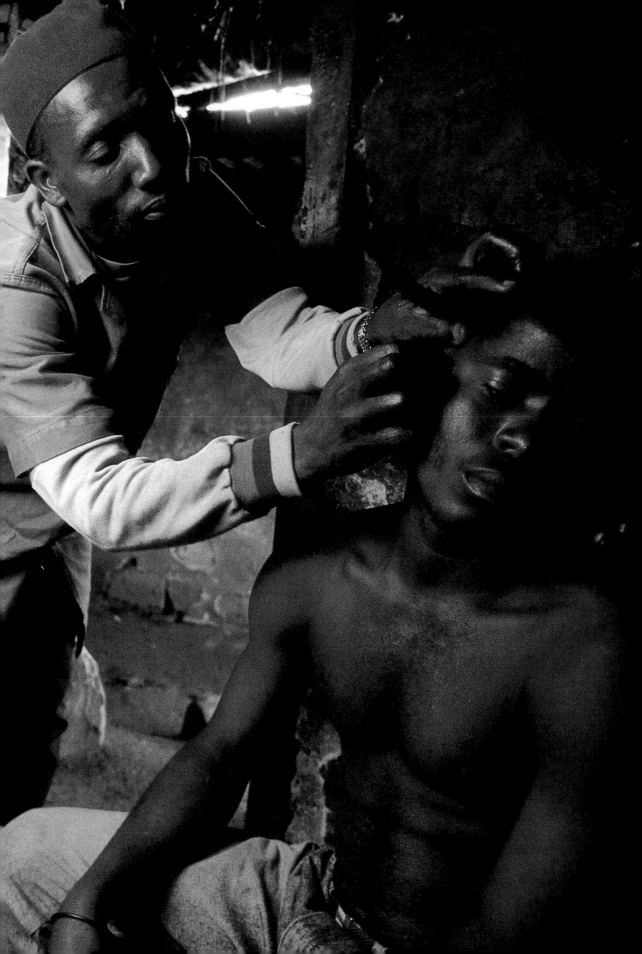

spring water. I gulped it thirstily. The liana was a reminder of another gift of the tropical forest—water in plentiful and consistent supply.

It may seem a contradiction, where rainfall is often measured in feet, that the water supply could now be a problem in some tropical regions. But such is the case in deforested areas. Without vegetation soil cannot absorb and retain heavy rainfall, then release the water gradually.

In the upper reaches of the Amazon and in Southeast Asia and India, for instance, deforestation has caused extreme variations in the flow of some rivers. At times too much water produces devastating flooding and erosion downstream. At other times too little water causes abnormally long dry periods. These changes have resulted in crop failures of increasing frequency.

I observed the effects of such deforestation on a smaller scale at Mount Oku in Cameroon. In the past at Oku a powerful *juju,* or spirit, called Mabu was able

Botanist Mike Fay (above) collects plants in the Central African Republic for study at the National Cancer Institute near Washington, D.C. Researcher Joseph Mbafor (above, right) extracts plant compounds in Cameroon. A remedy made from the inner bark of the **Enantia chlorantha** *(below) treats malaria.*

to protect the forest on the slopes of the mountain. Summoned by traditional rulers, he exhibited a fierce mask-visage, confronting anyone who dared cut the forest without permission. Nowadays Mabu's job is more difficult. Only remnants of that forest remain. And here, as in many parts of the tropical world, the large and growing population is putting ever increasing pressure on ever diminishing forest. People encroach to clear yet another sliver of land for food or for cash crops like coffee or potatoes. The fertility of the land is declining, as is the water supply.

John Parrott and his wife, Heather Macleod, came to Oku originally to try to save such endangered bird species as the Bannerman's turaco. "You start out thinking about bird conservation, and you end up focusing on potato cultivation," John told me. The Kilum Mountain Forest Project, sponsored by the International Council for Bird Preservation, centers on the remnant forest at Oku. The turaco serves as the project's symbol, but John and

Heather, the project coordinators, are also concerned with the needs of local farmers—for productive cash crops, good farming practices, and tree planting to conserve soil fertility and to prevent erosion. One of their most important goals is to educate local people about the role of the forest in sustaining the water supply. "You have to make people want to protect the forest," say John and Heather.

Wood is, of course, an obvious part of the forest's bounty at Oku. Woodcarvers in the region are known for their skill. Tangu Ngai Francis, who bears the honorific title *Nchinda*, is one of the most skilled. One evening at twilight I had climbed a long hill from the village to his house. The silken surface of a low stool drew my hand irresistibly. Short legs, whimsically carved into animals, supported the seat, perfectly shaped for comfort. "I get this wood from the nearby forest," Francis told me. His animal masks, both mythical and real, of elephants, antelopes, and monkeys seemed to take on life around us in the low light of evening.

In parts of Cameroon logging is a major industry. And tropical timber is big business worldwide. In 1988 tropical countries exported nearly 7 billion dollars' worth of hardwoods, not including finished wood products. These exports earn foreign exchange for many nations in Africa, in Latin America, and most particularly in Southeast Asia.

Beside the Ngoko River in southeastern Cameroon, the huge red logs I saw strewn across an open space easily exceeded in diameter my five feet eight inches in height. Here at Kéka the French logging company SIBAF—Société Industrielle des Bois Africains—has built for the duration of its logging concession a village complete with tidy houses for workers and foremen, an infirmary, and playing fields. From a long, low building came the cheerful babble of schoolchildren in classes.

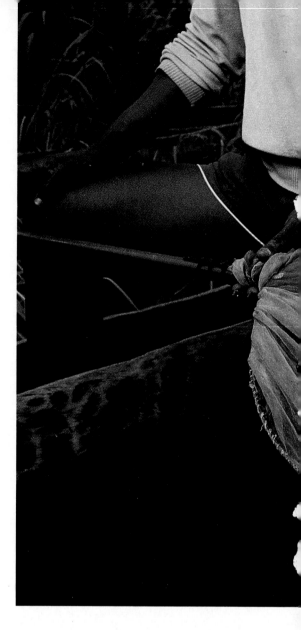

At the sawmill the air was filled with the shrieks of blades cutting into the logs fed along conveyor belts. Pierre Martineau showed me around. Front-end loaders tumbled logs down a slope into the Ngoko to begin their long journey to Europe. Men, balanced on floating logs, prodded other logs into place and chained them together into rafts. When the river rose, the rafts would float downstream to Brazzaville and to a railway that would haul them to ships bound for France. Because of the remoteness of this region and the high cost of transport, SIBAF practices high-grading, taking only the choicest trees of three of the most valuable species. "And the diameter has to be a minimum of a meter," Martineau said. By the time a high-quality log of African mahogany or sapelli—perhaps 25 feet long and 6 feet in diameter—is off-loaded at a French port, a year after being felled here, it will command well over $5,000. And its value will climb much higher when it is made into veneer for high-priced furniture.

In some parts of the world logging leaves deforested areas with little economic value for many decades. Some experts see sustainable harvesting of so-called minor forest products as a way of avoiding such deforestation. "A lot of us would argue that you shouldn't call them *minor* forest products," said Nels Johnson of the World Resources Institute in Washington, D.C., "because they are in some cases more valuable than the timber. I think we are just starting to learn the economics of nontimber forest products."

Charles M. Peters of the New York Botanical Garden in Bronx, New York, would agree. He and his colleagues were

among the first to seek a bottom line on those values. They have inventoried a 2½-acre plot of forest in Peru to assess the monetary value of its nontimber resources. It's true that the immediate income of about $1,000 from felling the timber in the study site might be greater than the estimated $425 that harvesting fruit, nuts, and rubber would bring. But the latter income could be earned annually; whereas the timber revenue would come only once. Dr. Peters acknowledges that his projections are subject to market fluctuations and that not every tract of the tropical forest has the same value.

There is another important aspect of the story—the social cost of cutting the forest. "There are millions of people in Amazonia making a livelihood out of extracting commodities from the rain forest and marketing them," said Peters. With deforestation these people would have no continued source of income.

Jewels of the forest, brilliantly colored butterflies have long attracted collectors to Africa, bringing hard currency to local economies. A harvester displays his catch at Mbaïki in the Central African Republic. Suppliers today breed some butterflies for export—a practice that may relieve pressure on endangered species.

Latex ribbons the trunk of a rubber tree in Malaysia. The tapper works at dawn, when latex flows fastest. Here a species native to Amazonia has been a plantation crop since the early 20th century.

Probably the major—and the best known—group of Brazil's extractive gatherers are the estimated 500,000 *seringueiros,* or rubber tappers. In the Amazon where it is native, *Hevea brasiliensis* is susceptible to a blight when crowded onto plantations. And so latex is still harvested in the wild. A skilled rubber tapper follows an *estrada*, a trail of rubber trees in the forest, skillfully slashing the bark of each tree to release the latex. During the dry season he might harvest and process 1,100 pounds of rubber, earning about 23 cents a pound and making a meager income. In the wet season he might turn to gathering Brazil nuts, which—because of intricate ecological interrelationships—are also difficult to cultivate successfully on plantations. But other Amazonian workers harvest dozens of other commodities less commonly known. These vary from hearts of palm and oil of the *Orbignya*—babassu palm—and rotenone, a pesticide from the root of *Lonchocarpus urucu*. In a recent

year the Brazilian government estimated that the worth of just a few such forest products ran to 86 million dollars. And that sum did not include the countless small transactions that go unrecorded.

In other regions of the tropical world—Southeast Asia, for example—overseas trade in rain forest products has flourished since perhaps the fifth century. These are as varied as boat caulking, paper finishes, aromatic oils, ginger, and birds' nests prized by Chinese gourmets.

Although much is already known about the riches of the forest, future possibilities are far more exciting. Plants still undiscovered, their uses untapped, may broaden the variety of food and increase its availability to mankind.

Bananas were once a rare sight; now the world consumes 40 million tons of them a year. And the once exotic avocado has become commonplace in the diet of many people. Yet, the world's tropical forests are home to hundreds of other kinds

of fruits, many of them important to local peoples but unknown to others. In the Kalimantan region of Borneo alone grow 17 species of mangoes, most of them marketed there. The names of Neotropical fruits such as *zapote, sachamangua, cupruçu,* or *camucamu* (the last contains 30 times the amount of vitamin C as an orange), or "mangosteen" and "durian" from Malaysia may one day roll off our tongues as easily as "banana" or "pineapple."

And the possibilities are not limited to fruit. Consider the winged bean, called "a supermarket on a stalk." This legume from Papua New Guinea may play in the tropics the role of the soybean in temperate zones, providing a protein source for these economically depressed regions of the world. Its leaves supply greens; its shoots, a vegetable like asparagus; its flowers, a delicate garnish. Its nut-flavored tubers contain three to four times the protein of potatoes and more than ten times that of cassava. A legume, it helps fix nitrogen in the soil. Such diversity may in the future offer possibilities for new food and economic well-being for the world.

D r. Michael Balick, director of the Institute of Economic Botany at the New York Botanical Garden, is hard at work discovering plant treasures in the tropical forest. "There are tens of thousands of edible species of fruits and leaves and vegetables, as well as roots and tubers, in these forests," Mike said, "yet in modern society we've narrowed it down to about 15 that keep us from starvation. In the rain forest the diet is much broader, more diverse."

Mike spends much of his time in Central and South America, but on this day we chatted in his office in the Bronx. "There are hundreds of oil-, latex-, and resin-producing species native to regions of the Neotropical rain forest," he told me. "Local people use them, but we don't. Now it is time to see what we can use."

Focusing on the palm family, almost a "tree of life" in some parts of the world, Mike explained that many of the members of this large family—which includes 2,000 species—have proved useful. Certain species are particularly important to indigenous peoples who rely on them for materials for hunting darts, for house building, for weaving, for charcoal, for medicines, and for a variety of foods.

It is a world of surprises for Mike. "I find one palm tree with a small red fruit, for instance," he told me. "We analyze it and find it has one of the highest concentrations of vitamin A in the plant kingdom." One genus of a palm native to Amazonia, *Jessenia,* Mike finds particularly intriguing. The fruit yields an oil with properties nearly identical to those of olive oil. The same palm also provides protein whose biological value is almost 40 percent higher than that of soy protein. *Jessenia* could prove to be a tremendous boon for developing countries while benefiting the rest of the world as well.

I did a little exploration for myself— on the shelves behind Mike's desk. A multitude of substances, objects, and packets of herbs attested to his ongoing and eclectic fascination with what comes from the tropical forest.

"Here's a nice story. The ivory nut palm," Mike said, picking up a small round nut with the soft yellow-whiteness of ivory. "Before plastic, many buttons were made of this. It takes a shine like elephant ivory. But you don't have to kill the source."

Mike then picked up a little jar. "This powder is from a vine of the Brazilian Amazon. Its fruit is 7 percent caffeine. Marketed in Beverly Hills, it's called Zoom—and it gives you a zoom!" (For those seeking the other extreme, a variety of coffee with almost no caffeine has been discovered on the Comoro Islands near Madagascar.)

Five kinds of caffeine-rich kola, shown here on their leaves, came out of Korup National Park in Cameroon. Kola nuts make up a prized trade commodity.

Our current use of Amazonian plants, Mike said, "represents only the tip of a huge beneficial iceberg of possibilities." That iceberg may eventually reveal solutions to such fundamental problems as sources of energy. The so-called petroleum nut tree in the Philippines, for example, produces an oil volatile enough for engine or cooking fuel.

One writer calls the tropical forest a "chemical storehouse." It is a storehouse particularly promising in medicine.

Some of that promise has become reality at a small factory in southwestern Cameroon where I found workers extracting substances from several local forest plants. Dr. Richard Ngengwe, chief pharmacist at Plantecam Medicam, pointed out large bins of bark stripped off *Prunus africana,* the African cherry, which would go into medicine used to treat prostate inflammation. "There are 20 different compounds in *Prunus*—no one works singly! We can't synthesize 20 compounds and get the same effect."

This pharmaceutical factory also

"Koko" break interrupts work on a plantation in Cameroon as a young worker chews cacao pulp. Fermentation and roasting give the seeds the chocolate flavor that earned the name "food of the gods." A machete-wielding harvester (above) severs a pod from a branch.

processes bark from the *Pausinystalia yohimba* tree, used as an aphrodisiac; seeds from *Voacanga,* for a heart tonic; and grains from *Strophanthus gratus*—Pygmy arrow poison—also for the heart. The concentrated extracts are very valuable for export to Europe, Dr. Ngengwe told me.

Perhaps chemical factory would be a better term than simply rain forest plant. One key to why plants in the moist tropics offer so much for modern medicine may lie in their competition for survival. Plants and animals here have developed, in intricate evolutionary adaptations, unique characteristics to ward off attack. Often that means they make toxic substances. Scientists concentrate on these compounds—called secondary metabolites because they are not necessary for growth or reproduction—to discover new substances for medicinal and other chemical uses.

P lants do marvelous things that human beings would never imagine," said Dr. Daniel L. Klayman, head of the Organic Chemistry Section at the Walter Reed Army Institute of Research in Washington, D.C. "We constantly read reports of newly discovered plant components whose chemical structures cause us to marvel at their novelty, their intricacy, and even their aesthetic beauty. Plant enzymes can do what chemists sometimes cannot, even by multiple steps in the laboratory. They enable the construction of complex molecules by the condensation of several kinds of chemicals. If these same individual chemicals were put in a flask, they would just sit there."

As we toured his laboratory, I looked at the wall-to-wall equipment: infrared spectrophotometers, nuclear magnetic resonance and mass spectrometers, high performance liquid chromatographs. Despite the power contained in such a lab, it cannot match some of the things that plants can do.

Walter Reed researchers are trying to find new substances, both naturally occurring and synthetic, to combat a perennial problem, malaria, especially new forms of the disease that are resistant to present-day drugs, some of them based on the original cinchona. Part of this effort requires evaluating folk remedies that use plant materials for the treatment of malaria and fevers. But rare is the Olympic gold success that came to researchers—Canadian and American—in the late 1950s when they discovered that the rosy periwinkle, a plant native to Madagascar's tropical forests, provides

substances that are successful in treating certain forms of cancer. "That sort of discovery comes perhaps every 20 years," Dr. Klayman said.

A young American, who ventured into the Amazon around the turn of the century to work as a rubber tapper, learned firsthand that medicines derived from tropical plants can save lives. He tells in his diary—recently brought to light by a grandson—a harrowing tale of the deaths of companions, of sickness. "This yellow fever is a terrible thing . . . unquenchable thirst . . . high fever . . . violent headaches . . . eyes and fingernails . . . yellow. The Indians would make tea from certain herbs which they would boil in a calabash shell. . . . The tea thus made looked exactly like ink and took me months afterwards to

Docked at Monte Alegre on the Amazon, boats take on bananas for market farther upstream at Manaus. Tropical forests abound in thousands of species of fruits and vegetables that could someday become as widely known as bananas.

get rid of the stains on my lips and hands, but it did me good."

The ill young man was not the first to notice that peoples of the forest have something to offer the world of modern medicine. From their first contact with the New World, Europeans took seriously some substances used medicinally by the people there. The well-known cinchona was borrowed by Jesuits from the Incas in 17th-century Peru. By the early 19th century the Brazilian ipecac root served in the treatment of amoebic dysentery. And from the hunters of the Amazonian jungle came the toxic compound curare—used on blowgun darts to bring down prey and now often employed as a muscle relaxant in surgery. We continue to use many such compounds, and the current quest for other medicinal substances is detective work on the grand scale.

Some of today's scientific sleuths operate in rooms filled with computers, such as I found at the College of Pharmacy, University of Illinois at Chicago. There I met Dr. Norman R. Farnsworth and some of his colleagues. To assist other researchers, they have developed a computer data base to search out information from all over the world, compile it, and make it available.

Other members of the scientific sleuthing team are detectives in the field who find specimens there and then

Forest turned into plantation in Cameroon produces palm oil for export. A harvester positions a 30-foot-long implement to cut a cluster of fruit. This palm species—native to West Africa and now grown throughout the tropics— provides two kinds of oil, one edible and one usually used in cosmetics and soap.

carefully collect and document them.

"So you're Q67B!" said Thomas McCloud, peering through a jungle of intricately twisted laboratory glass beakers and tubes filled with colorful liquids. He was addressing Mike Fay, who had brought me with him to the National Cancer Institute's facility in Frederick, Maryland. It was a bit like Stanley's "Dr. Livingston, I presume?" upon at last encountering his peripatetic quarry deep in Africa. Indeed, botanist Mike Fay, aka "Q67B" (his specimen collector's number), had come out of Africa. His objective had been plants that might possess a chemical key to treating some form of cancer or AIDS. "I always wondered who Q67B was when the samples came in," said McCloud, a researcher at the cancer institute. In an ongoing project NCI has sent more than 25 botanists to different areas of the world, particularly to

Worth warring over in earlier times,
spices of the rain forest still command high
prices. Workers in Madagascar (opposite)
dump vanilla pods into a steam box
for fermentation. In Indonesia a worker
(near left) strips bark from a tree
for cinnamon, later spread in the sun
to dry (below). Ripe pepper berries
(above) await harvest in Thailand.

the tropics. So far they have gathered 5,000 different plant species for the study. Mike collected more than 700 species in Africa.

A little later Q67B was pretty excited too. "That's one of mine!" he said picking up a little jar of pink powder. *Mousingi* is the plant's name in the Central African Republic where he collected it. In Latin it is *Uapaca heudelotii*. The computer readout indicated that this powder extract was one of several retrieved for closer scrutiny.

Other researchers, such as Dr. Richard Evans Schultes of Harvard, a leader in modern ethnobotany, look at what people use in their environment. Schultes lists more than 1,300 species "employed by natives in the northwest Amazon as medicines, poisons, or narcotics." And that list, he feels, is incomplete. In gathering this material highly trained ethnobotanists conduct painstaking interviews that probe lore and techniques of venerable traditional healers. They also collect voucher specimens to ensure correct identification.

Talking with botanists and ethnobotanists alike, I was aware of a sense of absolute urgency. As deforestation continues, species are rapidly disappearing. Not only are the *plants* disappearing but the knowledge traditional healers have of them is also at risk. Dr. Mark Plotkin of Conservation International puts it succinctly: "Each time a medicine man dies it is like an irreplaceable library burning down."

I traveled by air to the island nation of Madagascar, a land rich in endemic species and one of the most threatened botanical regions in the world. Below me the deforested hills and the eroding soil hemorrhaging into the Indian Ocean offered a vivid reminder of that sense of urgency.

"Madagascar's Gift to the World" were the *(Continued on page 106)*

Hunter in Congo displays his kill—a young lowland gorilla and a greater white-nosed monkey. The taking of "bush meat," while supplying protein for people in West Africa and in other tropical regions, may increasingly endanger some species.

With a chain saw a logger brings down a buttressed goliath in Congo, West Africa. Tropical hardwoods—for fine furniture, veneers, and other wood products—bring important, though often short-term, income to many rain forest countries.

words emblazoned on Dr. Nathaniel Quansah's T-shirt, together with a large pink flower—*Catharanthus roseus*—the rosy periwinkle. "Because of this plant four out of five children with leukemia are surviving, instead of four out of five dying, and more than half of the people with Hodgkin's disease live," said Nat, an ethnobotanist from Ghana working with the World Wide Fund for Nature.

The rosy periwinkle—that Olympic gold of medical research—has brought hope of more such finds. But because of population pressures, Madagascar is fast losing the remainder of its rain forests. "Last year I found 60 additional plants, mostly for medicinal use," Nat reported. He wants to convince local people of their own stake in preserving the forests—not for some far-off, sophisticated pharmaceutical miracle, but to have plants for their own traditional healing. "What I'm trying

Dugouts carry people and goods across the Oubangui River in central Africa. On the riverbank Ndolo Michel shapes a log into a canoe that will bring a good price. Craftsmen in tropical forests seek buoyant, rot-resistant wood for their boats, used for both transportation and fishing.

to do is appeal to emotions. You tell them that those plants they need come from the forest. And if there is no forest . . . ? They listen." Much of Nat's work is in rural areas. But even in the center of the capital, Antananarivo, there are opportunities to learn about traditional medicines.

Perhaps 80 percent of the world's people depend largely on traditional medical methods. Madagascar is no exception. On Friday the market was bustling, the stalls stacked high with vegetables and fruits. And in a corner not far off the street were tables covered with little bunches of plants for medicinal use. As Nat picked them up, the vendors, two women, patiently explained what each bunch of leaves, stems, or roots was good for. Nat then recorded local names and identified the plants by Latin nomenclature. Sometimes two or three different plants were used in combination. Burns, jaundice, dandruff,

venereal disease? The women had an answer. One leaned across the table with an air of confidentiality to show me three particular plants and to whisper that "used together they will help women's problems." The rosy periwinkle she singled out for liver problems. I left wondering. Perhaps on that table was some plant that would lead to a cure for another deadly disease.

What such a find might mean became more personal one day back in the States, when I spoke with Congresswoman Claudine Schneider of Rhode Island. "I learned I had Hodgkin's disease at the age of 25," said Schneider. One of the lucky ones then who survived, she is now healthy and is active in efforts to preserve the tropical forest—or "health treasure chest"—that provides so much hope for the health of others. "I only wish that . . . I had had the option of using the rosy periwinkle," she said.

Survival on a much broader scale, for all of us, may in some ways depend on another aspect of the bounty from these forests. And that is biodiversity. Within the tropical forest may lie important means of protecting the food sources of the whole world. The aim of agriculture has always been better crops and higher yields. In recent times, toward that goal, plant geneticists have developed strains of crop plants that have replaced traditional varieties, narrowing the genetic base. The newer, high-yield varieties are often genetically similar and therefore vulnerable to the same pests or diseases.

Mike Balick spoke of the importance of protecting wild relatives of genetically vulnerable crop plants, many of which have come out of the rain forest. How critical the genetic pool is became evident in the 1970s with the corn crop in the U.S. "The gene base was so narrow that when the corn blight came through the South it wiped out a substantial portion of the crop," Balick told me.

I spoke about this with Dr. Calvin Sperling of the Plant Sciences Institute of the U.S. Department of Agriculture. "For high productivity, disease resistance, and other desirable traits, plant breeders had developed improved hybrids," he explained. "Most varieties of corn were highly vulnerable to leaf blight fungus. Since they were developed at that time using the same ancestral parents, all derived from a few genetic lines. You may have had 20, 30, 50 varieties of corn, but they all had the same lineage and were all so similar that they had the same susceptibilities." Eventually scientists developed a blight-resistant corn to preserve future crops.

The lesson learned was an important one. Crops essential to human survival could be at jeopardy. And species that might be essential to saving those crops may well be in the world's tropical forests.

When sugarcane in the United States was hit in the 1920s by a virus spread by aphids, varieties of sugarcane from Java helped rescue the industry. In the 1970s the 3-billion-dollar coffee industry in Latin America was threatened by a fungus and was preserved by a resistant strain from Ethiopia.

As deforestation destroys species in the tropics, the genetic variation needed to protect an important crop may be lost forever. That is where the work of Sperling and crop geneticists worldwide comes in. Sometimes they collect the germplasm, which holds the genetic information for species and variations, in the form of vegetal matter and seal it in test tubes or freeze it to preserve it. This is not always successful. And, as Dr. Sperling explained, seeds don't always work. "Some species have what is known as recalcitrant seeds, which do not store well or resist germination after storage. They are short-lived, and dry out and die. In some cases the best way to store genetic resources is to keep them growing in the forest. There you can observe their relationships with pests, and the plants can continue evolving." Sperling is doing a survey of wild relatives of crop plants in a preserve in Ecuador.

The bounty of the world's tropical forests far exceeds our present-day understanding of it. But we do know even now that its value is incalculable. It exists in the knowledge that indigenous peoples have to offer us, in the forest products that enrich our lives today, and in the biodiversity and genetic variation essential to our future. The flora of the Amazon alone, insists Harvard's Schultes, "offers us an emporium . . . incredibly rich and varied and comprising thousands of genera of plants, some of which will have uses in the future that we today cannot imagine."

Nchinda Francis shows his sculpture— masks of animals and mythical creatures that appear in traditional ceremonies— in Oku, Cameroon. The artist also builds houses, furniture, and beehives. "If the forest be finished, we be finished," he says.

On a tree plantation in Malaysia, a crane hoists logs destined for export. Japan, a major consumer of tropical timber, buys about 44 percent of the world's exported harvest.

YANOMAMI TEENAGER ON THE HUNT, BRAZIL

Man and the

*"Equatorial forests, once unbroken belts of green, are rapidly
being clear-cut, strip-mined, drowned . . . , bulldozed,*

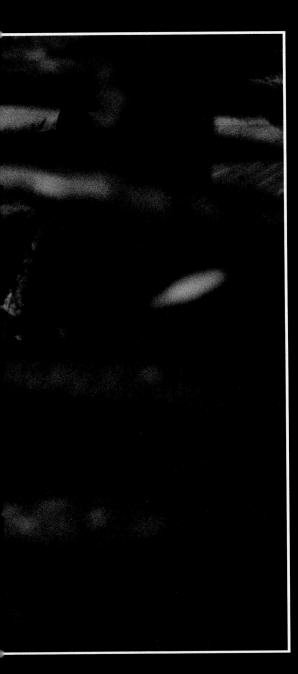

Forest

by
Tom Melham

J ust as the first man to eat an oyster was either very brave or very hungry, the first one to sample the tropical American plant known as manioc was either very smart—or soon very dead. For *Manihot esculenta* comes with a fatal flaw. Its potatolike tubers contain not only life-sustaining carbohydrates but also one of nature's deadliest poisons, cyanide. To eat manioc and survive, man first had to figure out how to avoid its venom.

He succeeded thousands of years ago, most likely using methods not much different from those employed today in the Amazon. Manioc tubers are peeled and grated or pounded into a pulp that is squeezed dry of its cyanide-rich juice, then heated to remove residual poison. Further processing gives rise to various solid and liquid foods, including tapioca, coarse flours, breads, even some alcoholic drinks.

Long after becoming an Amazonian staple, manioc went worldwide. Today it supports tropical populations around the globe.

Why should different tropical societies, especially those living within the rain forest's wondrously varied cornucopia, rely on the same potentially lethal plant? Despite its dangers, manioc offers great advantages. It grows in almost any soil, produces relatively high caloric yields throughout the year, and is easy to store (the tubers are simply left in the ground). While many other plants rapidly succumb to the rain forest's myriad insects, browsers, and agents of decay, manioc remains one of the region's most reliable and durable crops.

Among manioc's traditional cultivators, the Tukano Indians of northwestern Brazil and southeastern Colombia created more than ceremony when they first linked this plant to their marriage rites. Today as in the past, the Tukano consist of different language groups, or clans, and women must wed outside their clan. Tradition dictates they take along manioc as a sort of dowry. Since different clans often possess different strains of manioc, such exchanges foster dispersion and, eventually, genetic mixing. Thus, though knowing nothing of genetics, Tukano have for centuries encouraged the diversity and survival of their principal crop as well as of themselves.

Dr. Darrell Posey, an American ethnobotanist who has worked extensively with Brazil's Kayapó Indians, offers additional insight into existing relationships between tribal peoples and their rain forest environment:

"You might see a Kayapó walk along eating a mango, then casually toss the seed into the hole of a termite nest. Now, a termite nest makes for one of the most enriched soils in the rain forest. The chance of that seed coming up is perhaps a hundred times better than it is for one just thrown on the ground. Or take papaya; left on the forest floor, its seeds usually won't sprout. But drop them in some ashes, say in a burned-over spot of a Kayapó backyard, and there's a good chance they'll make it. These are not conscious acts; they're habits Indians follow simply because that's what has always been done. Many things you do, you do subconsciously, because it's part of your culture."

Subconsciously or not, forest tribes often interact so subtly with their environment that casual observers fail to see the human imprint. Dr. Anthony Anderson, an ecologist with Brazil's oldest institution for Amazonian research, *Museu Paraense Emilio Goeldi*, points up a fairly recent discovery.

"Charcoal remains, typically 8,000 to 11,000 years old, have been found over extensive areas of the Amazon, indicating that these areas were burned—sometimes over and over. Many sites contain ceramic shards, so man was present. There's an increasing array of evidence that indigenous groups manipulated plant resources in ways much more subtle than we once thought, over a much wider range of species. The idea that the Amazon has been totally pristine, like a museum for millennia, is pretty well shot full of holes."

Posey adds, "Many forested areas today are growing on top of old Indian villages, on charcoal-enriched 'black soils' developed through centuries of human presence. The Indians may be gone, but the forest that came up was put there—consciously or not—by them."

While scientists differ over the extent of impact wrought by indigenous humans on the forest, all agree that such groups have benefited continuously from their environment (Continued on page 121)

Isolated from the rest of the world for centuries, Brazil's Yanomami Indians face an increasingly uncertain future as outsiders invade and change their once remote homeland.

Islet of thatch in a green sea, a lone Yanomami house crowns a remote hilltop near the Brazil–Venezuela border. The dozen or so families it shelters survive by hunting, gathering, and farming. They move on every few years as local soils and prey animals become depleted.

Shopping as casually in the rain forest
as a city dweller in a supermarket,
a Yanomami mother and her children
(opposite) gather fresh produce for the day.
Forest plants and animals supply foods,
medicines, and herbs, as well as poisons to
stun fish and to tip six-foot arrows (left).
West Africa's Baka Pygmies, similarly
attuned to the forest, use leaves to shingle
their huts (above), and they rely on nets
fashioned from vines to trap prey (below).

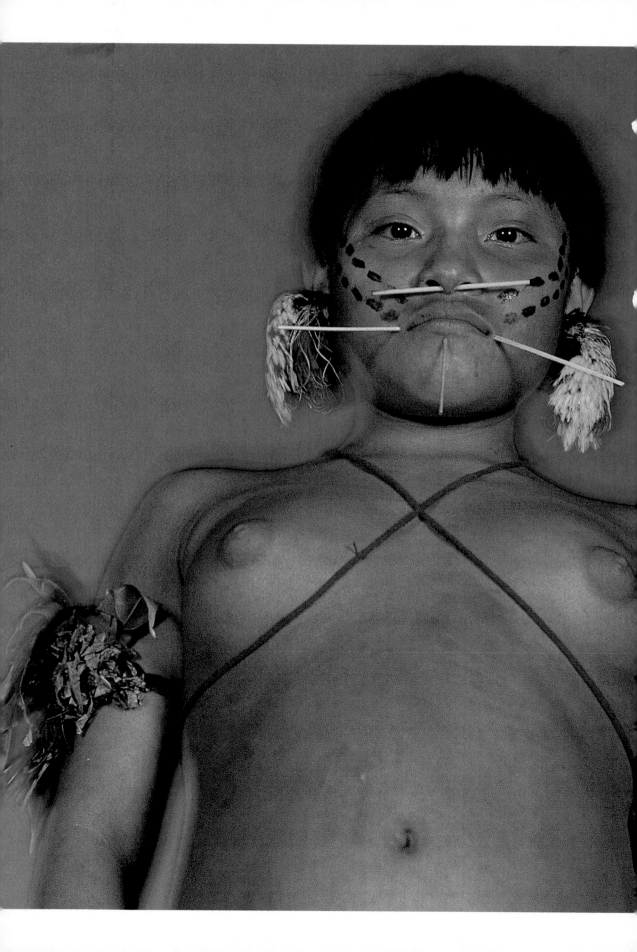

without eliminating it. In contrast, modern man—armed with his more powerful technology—has been far more destructive.

"Our ignorance of the Amazon is very great," admits Dr. Herbert Schubart, director of INPA, Brazil's National Institute for Amazon Research. "This is a huge river basin, the world's largest. Twenty percent of all river water flows here." The rain forest that cloaks much of this region qualifies as the biggest, most diverse, and least altered of any on earth. About 60 percent of the Amazon basin, nearly two million square miles, lies within Brazil. Says Schubart, "That is half the size of Europe. It is like a continent. But it is also a fragile ecosystem, and the soils often are poor."

Recent attempts to make Amazonia profitable have led to unprecedented rates of deforestation. As larger and larger areas are cleared, more forest species face extinction, soils erode, the land's productivity fades. Many scientists fear even more disastrous and wide-ranging results, from regional changes in rainfall to global warming, also called the greenhouse effect. In Brazil, says Schubart, "Deforestation trends we see now all were started in the last 20 years. Government took an active interest in 'developing' the Amazon; that means cutting the forest. Fiscal incentives were put in place." Tax breaks and land giveaways launched huge cattle ranches, mining projects, and—unofficially—land speculation schemes, all at taxpayer expense.

How much forest is being cut? Basing his estimate on satellite imagery, Dr. Philip Fearnside—an ecologist and research professor at INPA—puts current, annual deforestation in Brazil at nearly 8,000 square miles, about half the size of the Netherlands. Other experts estimate that the worldwide picture is six times as bad: About 50,000 square miles of rain forest

Forest plenitude furnishes a Yanomami girl with paloitos—*"little sticks"—for her face and with leaves, feathers, and flowers for her earlobes and her upper arms.*

disappear *each year*. Actual amounts are difficult to estimate and harder to verify. But today deforestation is accelerating and, many believe, out of control.

Equatorial forests, once unbroken belts of green, are rapidly being clear-cut, strip-mined, drowned (by enormous hydroelectric projects), bulldozed, and burned—all in the name of progress. To many it is nothing less than war on nature.

est—will solve their economic dilemmas.

So far, it's been an unrealistic hope, because most development schemes have mined the forest's riches, not harvested them sustainably. For a few years or even decades, these projects brought about a boom of activity and jobs; then the resource dried up and they blew away. Relatively few people gained, while the gulf between rich and poor widened. Even industry-rich Brazil suffered disappointment. Says Schubart, "What counts is money. We want to extinguish misery. Actually, Brazil's economy has been getting richer—but misery is increasing. This is what we are worried about."

Half the world away in Southeast Asia, logging has driven much of the export economy for years; lumbermen now expect the region's commercial stands of hardwoods to give out early in this decade. Today millions of once forested acres—nearly one-fourth of Southeast Asia's original rain forest—harbor plantations of rubber, palm, pulp trees, and other cash crops. While this agriculture is both exportable and renewable in varying degrees, it cannot duplicate the forest's rich bounty. It also leads to erosion and other permanent damage. Indonesia, for example, is relocating millions of urban and rural poor from overcrowded Java to other, still forested islands where most newcomers become subsistence farmers—often on soils unsuitable for farming. So far, these migrants have deforested some five million acres.

West Africa, beset by its own population pressures, has little original forest left except in Cameroon. African forests once were protected by difficult access and terrain, by high diversity of trees (which

Call it the Third World's War, since tropical forests happen to occur in economically depressed, developing countries of the Third World. Although some nations, like Brazil, are well on the road to industrialization, even these share much with the least advanced: rapidly increasing populations, widespread poverty, and a lingering conviction that development of their great natural resource—the rain for-

complicates mill operations), by laws limiting exports of whole logs. But populations in Nigeria, Côte d'Ivoire, and elsewhere are growing and hungry; cutting of both lumber and fuelwood intensifies, even on steep tracts, spawning erosion and impoverishing ancient forests.

Of all forested lands, Amazonia remains least affected by lumbermen, who have found its unsurpassed biological diversity dauntingly uneconomic and Brazil's ban on whole-log exports an added deterrent to profits. The coming collapse of Asia's commercial lumber industry, however, dictates rising values for Amazonian trees. Japan, which with the Netherlands dominates Southeast Asia's logging trade, is exploring new access routes to Brazil's untapped western forests.

Even without great foreign demand for wood, huge tracts of Brazilian rain forest continue to disappear. Some felled trees satisfy domestic lumber needs, but most never find their way to a sawmill or even a charcoal oven; transportation is so costly and the forest so extensive that untold billions of board feet are burned or allowed to rot each year. Philip Fearnside figures this annual waste to be in excess of a billion dollars, basing his estimate on retail lumber prices. The trees are felled simply to make room—mostly for ranches and farms—while mining operations, highways, and hydroelectric dams promise ever more development, ever less forest.

An equally damaging and even more pervasive cause of worldwide deforestation is the poverty-stricken peasant who relies on the forest for fuel and subsistence farming. As his numbers swell, so do the problems. Today's forests are disappearing as never before, largely due to exploding human populations and to contemporary attitudes toward nature and

Farming by machete (below) and fire (opposite), Yanomami use slash-and-burn agriculture to transform small forest tracts into temporary plots for manioc, potatoes, bananas, and other crops.

profits. In Brazil as in the U.S., for example, government traditionally· considers nature "raw land" as if it were unfinished, in *need* of change. Any human alteration instantly becomes an "improvement."

Similarly, early explorers labeled the Orinoco–Amazon forest a vast "green hell" and considered it an enemy, an unconquerable repository of mysterious, often noxious beasts and plants (and equally mysterious humans). Its miasmal danks were worthless but for the gold, spices, medicinal plants, and other portable treasures they held. Hardwoods were exploited, but very gradually; for centuries after their "discovery," rain forests remained more impediment than resource. Eventually man would find the machinery and the determination to clear them. Dr. Fearnside recalls, "At the Stockholm Conference in 1972, Brazil was the leader in denouncing any sort of suggestion that developing countries ought to control pollution or do anything to protect their environments. It even advertised in the *New York Times,* telling companies to locate in Brazil on the grounds that it had no pollution controls." Another instance of the development-at-all-costs attitude surfaced in 1988, when Amazonino Mendes, governor of Amazonas —Brazil's largest and wildest state— handed out chain saws to his constituency.

Certainly agriculture can seem a logical "improvement," what with the Third World's burgeoning population, its recurrent famines, and its increasing reliance on imported food. It's easy to gape at the rain forest's green torrent of life and attribute it to incredibly rich soils. But these soils are largely ancient and poor, denied mineral nutrients by their geology and the leaching effect of heavy rains for millennia.

The forest's lushness stems more from intense sunlight, bountiful rains, and a lack of winter than from fertile soils. Its year-round growth and year-round decay make for a rather reckless existence; in more temperate realms winter's seasonal slowdown allows organic matter to build up for the next growing season. Here all detritus is constantly and almost immediately recycled into living matter. Like a spendthrift forever splurging on new clothes, the rain forest never banks a dime. It is life lived ever at the brink.

Cut down the forest's absorbent cloak of trees and haul it off, and its nutrients go as well. Burn it and nutrient-rich ash may briefly benefit newly planted

Seed pod rattles encircle the ankles of tribal dancers in Cameroon, accompanying their exultant performance with a ratchety tattoo.

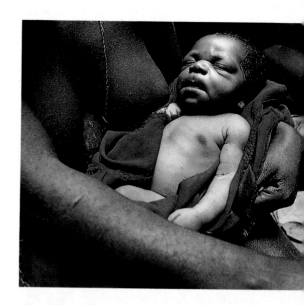

crops—or it may wash away with the rains, as will the now-bared land. Thin soils grow thinner, crop harvests grow poorer—unless the farmer turns to costly, usually unaffordable fertilizers.

All too often, rain forest nations have seen the forest as a quick fix for diverse economic ills. The Amazon has endured numerous booms and busts: sugarcane, rubber, bananas, ranching. In the mid-1980s Brazil's Polonoroeste project sought to make farmers of urban and rural poor by offering them land in Amazonian wilderness. While echoing the intent of the

19th-century Homestead Act in the United States, this and similar attempts at homesteading the Amazon have failed. Migrants usually lack expertise both in farming and in coping with the specific realities of life in the wilds. Government help has been slow and confused, at times failing to provide adequate funds, technical support, or market information. More than once, new farmers were relegated to areas with entirely inappropriate soils.

Dr. Christopher Uhl, a plant ecologist affiliated with Pennsylvania State University and EMBRAPA, Brazil's agricultural agency, criticizes such attempts, saying, "Brazil's national problems need to be resolved where they occur, when they occur, not here in the Amazon." He adds that even experienced peasant farmers "can be tremendously destructive; every year each one will clear three, four, maybe five hectares of forest for the main cash crop, upland rice. [One hectare equals 2.5 acres.] They get only one harvest, then put in manioc or some lesser crop—and start clearing more forest for rice. They prefer primary forest, burning it to get a good shot of nutrients to bring the rice into cultivation. But rice has a pitifully low price; they pay half their total production just to get it threshed. They're victims in a terrible economic situation."

As they suffer, so does the rain forest. Slash-and-burn agriculture predominates in Amazonia. Indians thrived on this timeless technique, but many of today's practitioners do not. INPA's Dr. Fearnside explains: "It depends on the scale. Practiced by indigenous peoples, who usually have low population densities, shifting agriculture is sustainable; land is left fallow 20 or more years and regenerates enough fertility and biomass to produce crops at the same level they were produced before. But if the cycle is accelerated—because population increases or because land is detoured to pasture and other uses—then it is not sustainable."

Uhl adds that current strategies "have been very *extensive*. Shifting agriculture uses huge amounts of land to support a single family over a lifetime. Many pastures have a ridiculously low carrying capacity. My feeling is that all approaches need to be much more *intensive*—whether it's lumbering *(Continued on page 133)*

Life's joy and death's sorrow at once grip a Baka tribe as it buries a woman who died in childbirth (left)—and welcomes her surviving newborn to the fold (top).

Helicopters and chain-sawed clearings foreshadowed the coming of miners to Brazil's Yanomami country. Such arrivals not only despoiled forest and tribal cultures but also exposed Indians to often fatal diseases.

Brazil's forest Indians quickly adopt trappings of civilization. A Kayapó (opposite) mixes contemporary regalia with traditional; a Yanomami mother looks at life anew (right), and children show off a Rio-inspired towel (below).

or cattle or farming, as opposed to extensive uses that gobble land irresponsibly."

Though much of Amazonia is best suited to forestry and agroforestry, Uhl says, "Some parts should be devoted intensively to agriculture. The floodplain forest—a fairly narrow strip of fertile land flanking major Amazon drainages—has tremendous potential for rice and grain production, fish culture, and other activities. It has rich sediments from the Andes. If it were in southeast Asia, it would have a flourishing economy. It's crazy that Belém [Amazonia's largest city, near the river's mouth] gets almost all its food from São Paulo"—about 1,500 miles away.

As with any development proposal for the rain forest, however, a caveat: Proceed with caution. Dr. Richard O. "Rob" Bierregaard, an American ecologist with a decade of Amazon research, explains that natural floodplain forest already generates much for man. It produces not only forest fruits and root crops but also the Amazon basin's chief source of protein: fish. More than 2,000 species inhabit the watershed,

and many, he explains, are fruit-eaters dependent upon the produce of river-edge trees. "When you turn that forest into rice fields and pastures, you take away the fishes' food—and undermine the major protein source for a lot of the population. We need to protect river-edge forest, to maintain the river ecosystem."

Of all development schemes currently pursued in Brazil, Uhl says, cattle ranching ranks among the worst, in some ways the most wasteful. It began with hopes of imitating agricultural successes of the U.S. and Argentina; Brazil's government offered huge allotments of forestland to would-be cattlemen, who earned an additional acre of land for every three they cleared. Says Uhl, "It was a system to clear, clear, clear, driven simply by the desire to gain control of as much land as possible, as quickly as possible."

But things started to go sour for many ranchers—as they had for farmers. Pastures lost fertility after a few years, despite follow-up burnings of new growth. Hooves compacted the thin soil, leaving it less and less productive, causing cattle to need more and more acreage. Severe overgrazing left some tracts nearly useless for any sort of agriculture. Despite such failures, Uhl maintains, "You *can* have sustainable pasture in the Amazon. The impediments are not technical. The real question is economics—*should* it be done? Are people creating pastures because they seriously want to be *fazendeiros* [ranchers], or do they have another agenda?" Such as land speculation.

Anderson agrees: "The Amazon is a big place; to prohibit all ranching would be foolish. But it's homogenizing the landscape. What's needed is to stop expanding so much, to consolidate areas already under pasture, and integrate them with other things, creating a patchwork."

Some compare overgrazed former forestlands to moonscape, fostering the impression that such impoverished lands can never again support any useful growth. But, says Anderson, this once cut, forever-gone image of the rain forest "just isn't true. It *is* possible to reintroduce a forest."

Adds Uhl, "You don't turn rain forest into desert. If you really abuse the land for a long time, you might get something like what in Wisconsin or Michigan is called an 'old field'—a community of weedy grasses that's quite stable and rather difficult for trees to invade. Such 'old field' systems are very flammable, so fire becomes a big factor in maintaining them."

Once protected from fire, however, these degraded areas usually regain forest cover. "It won't be primary forest," Uhl explains. "You're not going to have whatever it was that took 5,000 years to develop. But you will get something that functionally behaves very much like forest. Very quickly you'll get leaf cover; in three or four years the leaf biomass will be about the same as the original forest's. You'll have the same evapotranspiration, the same water processing and radiation processing, the same amount of light absorbed or reflected back into the atmosphere—the kinds of things that might influence regional or global climates. Within five years you'll have a functional ecosystem, possibly a more efficient one in terms of nutrient retention than the original."

Some deforested areas, however, never recover. Hydroelectric dams permanently flood huge expanses, and such projects are booming in Brazil. José Antônio Muniz Lopes, director of planning and engineering of Eletronorte, the government utility that provides electricity to Amazonian Brazil, told me, "Hydroelectric potential for the Amazon basin is about 100,000 megawatts." That's enough to power ten cities the size of Washington, D.C.

"We have 5,000 megawatts in use or near use now," he continued, "and we'll double that by the year 2000." Those 10,000 megawatts—the combined output of ten projects—are ideal, peak-use figures; in reality the average output will be more like 5,000 megawatts. The official cost of the projects, Muniz added, will be about ten billion dollars, though critics claim actual costs will total more than twice that much. And Muniz plans to harness the 90,000 megawatts remaining.

Throughout the world, hydroelectric projects are considered "clean" alternatives, often preferable to oil, coal, or nuclear power plants. But much of the Amazon basin, especially the downstream, Brazilian portion, is fairly flat; tributaries often lack the necessary drop needed for efficient power generation, and mistakes have been made. Balbina, a billion-dollar dam blocking the Uatumã River north of Manaus, is a case in point.

I flew over Balbina with Rob Bierregaard late in 1989, after Eletronorte had approved, then canceled, a surface visit. From the air it looked like a U.S. Army Corps of Engineers postcard, the dam a streamlined concrete plug fronting a modest-looking lake. The largest hydro project in wild Amazonas state, it oozed "progress" as it testified to the nation's commitment to modernize, industrialize, and above all to develop its forests. Yet the image was flawed. The vast sprawl of trees framing its lake was gray and nearly leafless. Half a million acres of primary rain forest stood dead or dying, drowned by the dam's now-risen waters. The open "lake" we'd seen was but a tiny portion of an immense yet shallow reservoir that, over most of its expanse, held only several feet of water. Enough to kill trees but not cover them. Few had fallen; the forest remained nearly as dense in death as it had been in life.

Scattered across this gray sea lay some 1,500 green islands, hilltops of living forest that survived thanks to slightly higher elevations. Though they appear healthy, "biologically they're almost worthless," Rob said. Since 1979 he and others have studied rain forest fragments, chunks of primary forest isolated from each other by ongoing clear-cut operations. They found that subdividing rain forest does not produce viable miniatures of continuous forest; instead, fragmentation can cause a permanent loss of species, because animals—even many birds—are loath to cross cleared areas.

"It's surprising how a little break in continuity can create a major barrier to animal movement," Rob said, recalling one study area that had been separated from continuous forest by a swath only 80 yards wide. "Before that cut was made, I figured it would do nothing. I knew some birds had part of their territory in what would become the fragment, part in the continuous forest, and I thought they'd just come and go—it wouldn't be a big deal for a bird to fly 80 yards. But after isolation most birds left the fragment and wouldn't come back, though it was still their territory. I guess it's like someone putting a superhighway through your backyard."

In effect even a narrow surround of clear-cut isolates forest creatures almost as completely as a watery moat or a sky-high fence. This realization has implications throughout the Amazon, for it makes every road and reservoir a potential barrier to wildlife. Each is also a conduit for deforestation, points out Fearnside.

"Hydroelectric projects affect much more land than what they flood. Roads are built to all dams, which often are in remote places, and those roads bring in people who cut the forest, to farm or whatever." Balbina, he adds, "is a disaster in every respect—environmentally, financially. Its human impacts are tremendous."

It also is a waste of the living forest, for its dead trees yield no lumber or even charcoal. Less than 2 percent of the reservoir area was selectively logged before flooding, basically the damsite and "lake" bed. Ongoing decay of the drowned forest generates methane, hydrogen sulfide, and other products deadly to aquatic life. Balbina's stagnating waters do make a perfect brood home for mosquitoes, however, thus promising to reinforce Brazil's position as malaria capital of South America. One more problem: Despite the huge area inundated, not enough water exists to

Ravaging the forest for gold's glimmer, Brazilian garimpeiros—miners—assault a once wooded and fertile riverbank in Amazonia with hydraulic dredges (opposite). Pumps lift the muck to a sluice box, which traps heavier particles while lighter ones pass through in a torrent (above). Workers concentrate the box's gold-laden sediments by adding mercury (left), a deadly pollutant that taints the air, the land, and the water as thousands of miners invade Amazonia's remotest realms.

push all of the dam's turbines all the time.

Says Fearnside, "There's virtually nothing on the positive side; other dams also flood big areas, but most of them at least produce a significant amount of power. Balbina doesn't. Its watershed is so small that rainfall won't keep the dam's five turbines turning more than one month out of the year." Average water flow, he says, barely powers two of Balbina's 50-megawatt turbines. "That means only 100 megawatts produced on average, not the projected 250 [for five turbines]. Even before they started building it, Eletronorte engineers calculated it would provide just 112.4 megawatts, average output. Transmission losses cut that to 109 megawatts at Manaus—which is a tiny amount of energy, considering that it has cost about a billion dollars. And then there are all the environmental impacts."

Tucurui Dam on the Tocantins River in eastern Amazonia has a reservoir roughly as big as Balbina's. But when completed, it will generate 4,100 megawatts average output, says Muniz—nearly 40 *times* as much power for the same level of environmental destruction.

Fearnside adds that as early as July 1986 Eletronorte's president admitted that Balbina was a mistake. But Muniz, one of the project's designers, remains adamant. "It was the right thing at the time. There were no alternatives," he told me in 1989. He declined to say how many more dams the utility contemplates for Amazonia.

"The full plan is 80 dams," counters Fearnside. "Not the six to be built by the year 2000, which Eletronorte emphasizes. Or the 18 dams listed in its 2010 plan. It's 80—which would flood about 39,000 square miles."

Eyes fixed on the balance, a miner weighs out his week's take—143 grams of crude gold, worth about $1,400. Hired hands share in the bounty, but with cantinas pricing 25-cent cans of beer at two grams each ($20), few mining camp residents keep their gains for long.

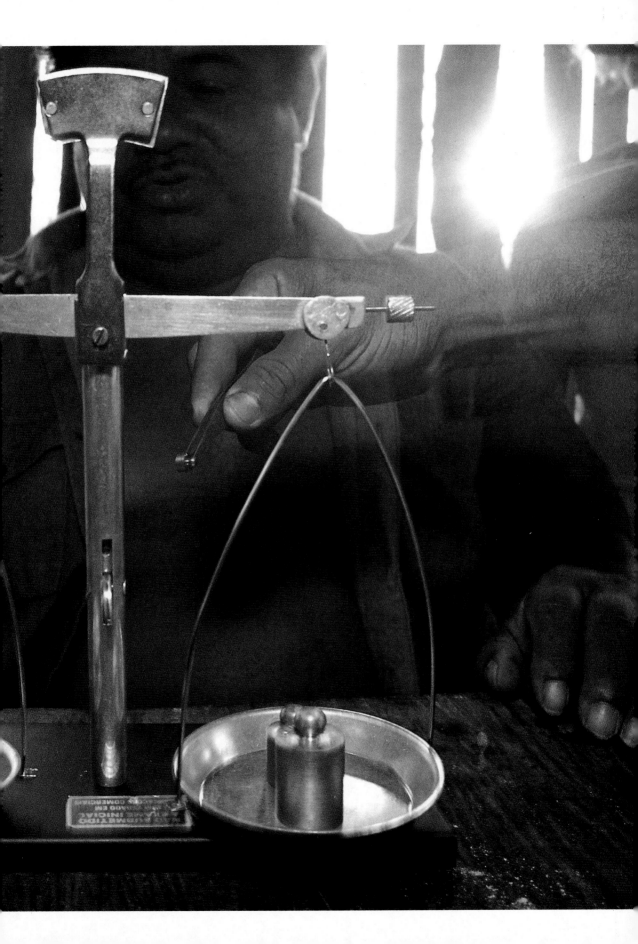

One of those projects, nearing completion when I visited in 1989, is Samuel Dam, in Rondonia state. Its reservoir, like Balbina's, is shallow, expansive, and dominated by stands of gray, dead trees. Dam personnel, however, talk with pride of a program that relocates wildlife isolated by the reservoir's rising waters. A video clip continuously on view in the Manaus airport shows relocation crews maneuvering skiffs through Samuel's bleak forest, wrestling marooned animals out of treetops, then releasing them onto drier ground—while the audio boasts of saving "our rain forest." It's good public relations, especially since the airport is international, and Manaus ranks as Amazonia's unofficial capital. No doubt the crews are sincere. But

such capture-and-release programs "are ridiculous, a waste of time," says Rob Bierregaard. "Crews take anything they can find, tear sloths and monkeys out of trees, then just let them go at the base of the dam. The animals run into the forest, where there are already plenty of sloths and monkeys, and in come another hundred. Dumping animals into territories of other animals is *not* a good thing to do."

Crowding means intensified competition, affecting not only introduced species and the plants and animals on which those species normally feed, but also nearby niches occupied by other, normally independent species, each with its own biological web of dependents. Given the rich diversity and plentiful interrelation-

ships of rain forest biology, crowding can set off any number of chain reactions, going any number of ways. And so it seems Brazil's numerous hydroelectric projects are not as environmentally "clean" as once presumed. But the nation needs power if it is to sow Amazonia with cities and industry and exploit the basin's enormous natural wealth.

Ironically, though Amazonian soils generally are mineral poor, Brazil itself is incredibly rich in mineral resources.

Monument to modern demands, an oil derrick tops a dynamited, bulldozed ridge in Papua New Guinea. Such camps rely totally on helicopters; bubble ports (left) enable pilots to see beneath their craft.

Carajás, in the eastern Amazon, holds 30 percent of the world's high-grade iron ore, the largest such deposit on earth. Other Brazilian sites claim important reserves of aluminum, tin, and copper, as well as strategic metals such as tungsten, molybdenum, and uranium. In addition the country contains precious metals and gemstones, all of which lure mining companies and *garimpeiros*—the Brazilian equivalent of sourdoughs—to explore and exploit the Amazon. Their wanderings increasingly bruise the forest, often causing long-term and even permanent changes.

Strip-mining disrupts rain forest, of course; overlying trees must be bulldozed to get at the ores below. But damage often extends far beyond the ore-bearing lode, for mines—like dams—spark road-building and other activities that inevitably come at the forest's expense. Then there are concerns about pollution.

So far, mining and loading operations at Carajás have earned generally high marks from environmentalists. But a 62-billion-dollar, second-stage development scheme, the Grande Carajás Program, or PGC, has sparked tirades of protest. PGC envisions the construction of 34 pig-iron smelters, iron-alloy plants, and cement factories—all powered by charcoal. On top of the infrastructure necessary for these facilities (and the resultant clearing of forest), the operation implies an enormous need for wood. Fearnside figures that 20 pig-iron smelters will burn about 2.4 million tons of charcoal yearly—more than 10 million tons of wood. Anderson projects PGC's annual needs at more than 15 million tons, which he equates to nearly 600 square miles of standing forest. Both are concerned about where that charcoal will come from. PGC planners insist that only sawmill scrap and plantation trees will fuel the charcoal kilns; but, says Fearnside, "Charcoal is likely to come from accessible native forest as long as such forests exist."

He points out that Amazonia's high

transportation costs encourage pig-iron producers to fell nearby trees rather than bring waste wood from distant mills. Fearnside also questions why PGC's administrative region should span some 350,000 square miles, an area more than twice the size of California. Much of it is forested.

Turning rain forest to charcoal for smelting not only destroys trees but also pumps huge amounts of carbon dioxide and other greenhouse gases into the atmosphere, contributing to global pollution and possibly accelerating the warming trend observed through this century. That could cause alterations in regional climates and ocean currents, which in turn would disrupt agriculture and fishing worldwide. While the burning of fossil fuels remains man's major contribution to atmospheric carbon (with the U.S. and the USSR contributing a third of the world's total), incinerating forests also aggravates the situation. Yet developers march on.

"The problem is that there's so much forest here, and it's all free," says Fearnside, adding that Grande Carajás is a study in false economics. Not only do its developers receive generous tax subsidies but they also pay nothing for standing trees they use. In effect government treats the forest as worthless. Only through such practices can the project mine, smelt, and ship pig-iron at a profit, for the metal's international price remains low. "It's crazy— government is *(Continued on page 147)*

Seeking to ease pressures on overpopulated Jakarta (opposite), Indonesia offers land to transmigrants who leave Java to resettle on less developed islands. Embarkees (below) bound for Irian Jaya—New Guinea—take plant stocks and hopes of a new life.

*Wandering scar of development
cleaves primary forest in Indonesian
Borneo. This road, built to convey
transmigrating farmers and
their crops, encourages further
settlement—and destruction.*

throwing away forest, a potentially useful resource, and subsidizing pig-iron with tax incentives that all taxpayers in Brazil pay for. For the businessmen who own these projects, of course, it's a good deal."

One Brazilian mining executive told me that when it comes to business in Brazil, "Everything has to be huge. Ten percent profit is nothing. Here, if you can't make 100 percent profit, you don't do it."

Wide profit margins, some say, are needed in a country where annual inflation in 1989 exceeded 1,200 percent. And doesn't a company's high profitability ultimately benefit the nation through income taxes and economic growth? Not lately. In recent years Brazil has so ardently wanted its Amazon developed that it allowed min-

ing companies, ranches—almost any businesses—tax-free status for their first ten years, with the possibility of renewal. The mining executive noted one exception: "We pay a tax on mineral exploitation," a user's fee, really, designed to compensate the nation for depleting its ores. "It's very low, something like 3 percent." Yet even this nominal tax never gets to the federal treasury, he added, since the government gives the company tax credits for meals and other services it provides its workers. Thus Brazil not only gives away its vast mineral deposits but also heavily subsidizes the exploiters. Relatively few jobs or other economic benefits result, because most mines are strip mines, which are mechanized and not labor intensive. The

Poor planning spells disappointment for transmigrants to Borneo, where seasonal rains can turn a costly new road like the one opposite to impassable mud; thin soils make for meager yields (above); new towns (right) spawn severe erosion.

chief beneficiaries of Brazil's natural wealth and governmental largesse remain the company owners.

Another sort of mining in Brazil distributes economic gains more equitably, because it is laborious, not dominated by corporations, and its resource is so widely scattered: gold. Tens, perhaps hundreds, of thousands of gold miners have been working Brazil's Amazon, usually in small groups. They seek not hard-rock ore, locked up in stony veins, but alluvial deposits—fine flakes that Amazonia's many

rivers continually erode and scatter, then accumulate in one bend or another. Such caches are unpredictable, ever changing, and spread over a huge area; periodic floods suddenly wash them away (or cover them up) and lay bare previously hidden bonanzas with equal ease. Which is why, though the Amazon has known five centuries of miners, its rivers still hold a lot of gold.

Like California's 19th-century prospectors, today's garimpeiros rely on time-tested gold pans and sluice boxes. No

just as gold caches come and go. Since garimpeiros hew fairly close to a river's course, their impact on rain forest—especially interior stretches—seems almost benign, compared with that of strip mine operations such as Carajás. Certainly it is less dramatic. But in fact it can be far worse. Gold miners physically disrupt not only river bottoms but also banks and floodplains—important to soil fertility and aquatic life. The mobility of balsas and dredges enables them to wreak havoc over a gigantic area, unlike localized strip mines. And there are chemical concerns; Brazil's gold miners continually sow the seeds of impending ecological disaster.

Yeah, it's one of my all-time favorites," George said sardonically as he watched me add powdered orange drink to a bucket of river water. "Mercury, diesel fuel, and Tang, all mixed together."

Actually, he'd left out a few other ingredients: Plastic trash, food scraps, detergents, and human sewage also tainted the water—all contributed by miners working just upstream from our campsite on the Uraricoera River in Roraima state, north central Brazil. We drank it, not out of ignorance but necessity; bottled water had been promised but never supplied. Already we'd been on the Uraricoera several days and would remain several more. Daily loss of liquid in the tropics had brought us to the point where drinking nothing posed a much bigger and more certain danger—dehydration—than did the risk of imbibing critical amounts of mercury or some intestinal bug from the river's polluted but fast-moving waters.

mules, however. The region's flat and watery expanses recommend other transport, primarily *balsas*—pontooned and covered rafts that serve as houseboat, dredge, and sluice box all in one. They ply the rivers, mooring over promising sites and relying on divers or mechanical dredges to vacuum bottom muck up to on-board riffles that sift and hold heavier sediments, including gold flakes, while the chaff gushes back to the stream. Balsas work alone or lashed together in banks; they may stay weeks in one area or disappear overnight,

George, a soldier of fortune with a yen for colored diamonds, was investigating the area's gemstone potential and serving as my guide and translator. The Uraricoera was remote; until garimpeiros began arriving, mostly in the last decade, this region had been a near-total wilderness of primary rain forest. Even when we visited in 1989, its banks boasted no cities, not even villages. But balsas and shore-bound cantinas punctuated the river, outboard canoes skimmed its surface, and *pistas*—crude airstrips hacked through nearby forest—assured supplies of food and other necessities. Miners often stayed months at a time; all their castoffs, from gummy oil filters and worn-out engine parts to everyday garbage and spilled mercury, wound up in the river. It was laundry tub, sewer, and trash can.

Of all the miners' leavings, mercury, notoriously toxic and long-lived, presents the worst threat. Miners process their ore with it; though alluvial gold can be mechanically separated from dross—by panning, for example—Amazonia's gleaming flakes often are so small and widely scattered that after a trip through sluice box and pan, much waste remains. The simplest way to separate the two is to add mercury, which amalgamates the gold, then to pour off the liquid mercury-gold mixture from the remaining grit. Finally, the amalgam is heated to vaporize its mercury, leaving a hard gold button. Carefully done, the process can recycle almost all of the mercury. But garimpeiros are not the most careful of men; spills occur, most miners use more mercury than needed, and few try to recover what they burn off. Quicksilver's cost is small compared with gold's value. Yet such carelessness increasingly poisons the ecosystem, for vaporized

Sick with malaria, a settler's four-year-old endures in Ariquemes, Brazil—reputed world capital of the malady that afflicts 90 percent of the town. Forest Indians, lacking natural defenses against this introduced disease, similarly fall prey.

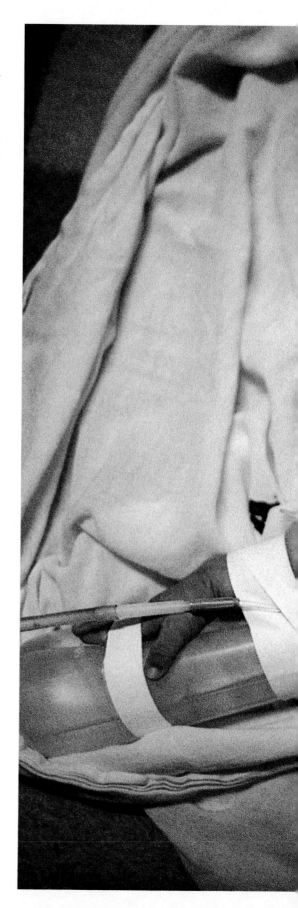

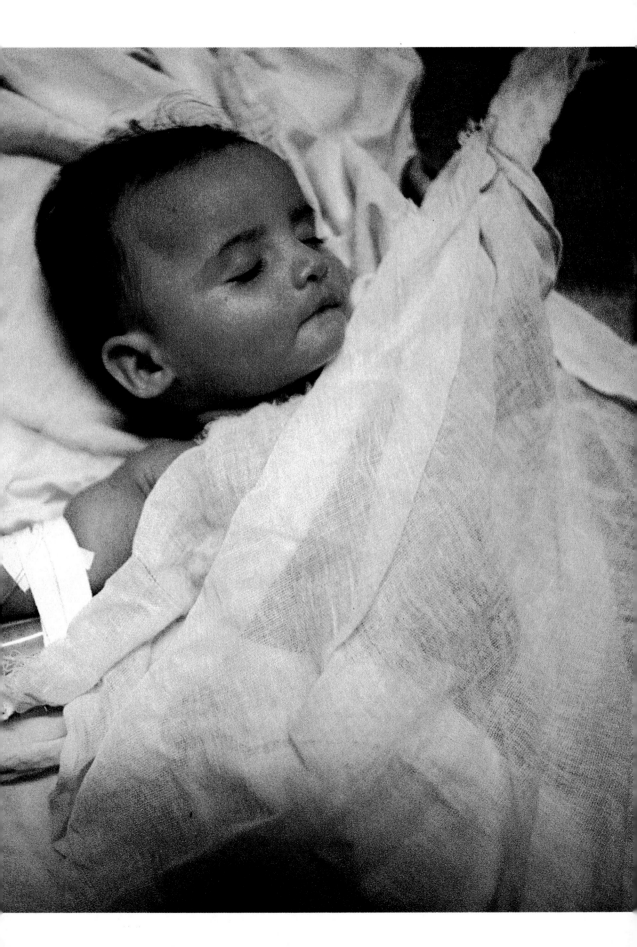

mercury readily condenses, returning to land and leaf and river in an unseen fog of tiny droplets.

Animals and people absorb the odorless and invisible fumes, which can cause nerve and brain damage over time. Mercury is heavy. It accumulates in river mud and then is ingested by various bottom feeders that in turn pass it up the food chain, eventually to the ultimate consumer, man.

"Mercury is a very serious public health problem in Brazil," says Fearnside. "People aren't feeling the effects yet because it takes many years to get started. Brazilians eat a lot of fish, and the cheapest species, the ones most important to the poor, are the most contaminated."

One regional study in Brazil estimates that 86 tons of mercury have been released into a single watershed. But no one really knows how much is in the Amazon, or where. No accurate tallies are kept of mercury or gold sales, the latter officially illegal but actually widespread. Nor is there a garimpeiro census; estimates run from 25,000 to 150,000 gold miners, just in Roraima. Whatever the real numbers, a lot of miners are dumping a lot of mercury, and their high mobility enables them to contaminate huge areas in a relatively short time. Alluvial gold is where you find it; each new discovery sets off another rush—and another influx of mercury.

Often, the garimpeiro's lust for gold has taken him illegally into protected areas, such as national parks and indigenous reserves (set aside for native tribes). A major chunk of the Uraricoera River basin, for example, lies within the bounds of a declared reserve for the Yanomami Indians—yet when I visited in late 1989, the

river area was aswarm with pistas and balsas and cantinas. One miner candidly admitted his intrusion: "I know I'm inside an Indian area, doing things Indians don't do. But it is not illegal, because I paid the Indians a percentage, and they accepted it. Whenever they need this land, I will go away to someplace else."

Huge in size and thinly populated, indigenous reserves lack effective border patrols. Occasional skirmishes between Indians and garimpeiros have resulted in injury, death, even dismemberment, but most miners I met claimed to be on friendly terms with local *indios*. They talked of giving Indians food, medicines, and other supplies they otherwise would not get, of paying Indians to hunt for them or to show them gold-bearing areas. Many sincerely believed they were the Indians' best friends, and some Indians concurred.

I especially recall one grinning local chieftain showering warm greetings on newly arrived garimpeiros while his hand held their offering: a tumbler full of whiskey.

Dr. Alcida Ramos, an anthropologist at the University of Brasília who specializes in the Yanomami people, warned me, "The situation is explosive. Today some Indians and garimpeiros may seem like friends. But that friendship can end in a minute. Some places, there are no animals in the forest, because garimpeiros hunt them and their planes scare them away. There are no fish in the rivers because of

Placid surface of Brazil's Balbina Dam reservoir (opposite) masks enormous ecological damage. It drowned half a million acres of forest yet made little use of the doomed trees (below), whose ongoing decay fouls the watershed.

the pollution. The Indians have to go to the garimpeiros for protein. And they resent it."

With or without bullets, with or without intent, garimpeiros are killing the Indians. Even well-meaning miners hasten the demise of native traditions, simply by their presence. They bear the trappings of a very different, profit-oriented life-style. They bring mercury and disease. Malaria and measles and influenza, all imported to Amazonia from distant lands, today rank among the top killers of Brazil's Indians.

Nowhere has the clash of cultures been more evident than at a red-dirt pista called Paapiu, gouged from jungle green near the Mucajai River in Roraima state. When I arrived in October 1989, one end of it was flanked by mining's paraphernalia: rough-hewn barracks and cantinas, workshops, planes and helicopters, all in various stages of repair. Pilots, prostitutes, and cooks mingled with garimpeiros, who worked mostly for several middle-size mining companies, seeking gold and cassiterite, an ore of tin.

Near the pista's other end, not 200 yards away, a monumental thatched cone rose eerily above the surrounding scrub forest with all the drama and timelessness of a Giza pyramid. It was the roof of a Yanomami lodge. Just outside stood eight or ten visiting Mucajai Indian women, nude save for their *tangas* (string girdles), and all smiles as they painted stripes, zigzags, and delicate stylized flowers on each other's skin. They were so happy, so full of childlike delight and innocence in the bright sunlight.

Invited inside the lodge, I stepped through its low portal—and passed from full sun abruptly into a black hole. I could see nothing in the windowless lodge except several narrow streaks of sunlight jabbing down from minor roof holes. The air was smoky and still. No Mucajai laughter, only wheezy groans and mutterings punctuated the black silence; as my eyes slowly adjusted to the dimness, I saw them: 50, maybe 70, Yanomami of all ages, most

flung into hammocks or upon the dirt floor, as if dead. They were not dead, merely *los condenados*, the damned. Occasionally one would rise up slightly, fix me with a vacant stare or accept a tidbit of food offered by a neighbor, then flop back. Few could stand. One who did: an anguished mother struggling beneath the weight of her unconscious son, whose body stretched from her neck nearly to the ground. Toddlers with bloated stomachs wandered among dazed adults and withered crones in a scene of Dantean suffering—all of them broken, seemingly without hope, the opposite of the jolly Mucajai just outside. Their curse was malaria—malaria brought by the garimpeiros and gone untreated thanks to governmental mismanagement. And as if this agony were not enough, every few minutes the roar of a plane landing or taking off filled the air, making conversation, even thought, temporarily impossible. Paapiu's pista, only yards from the lodge, witnessed more than 50 takeoffs and landings that day, making it Roraima's busiest "airport" by far, outstripping even the international airport at Boa Vista, the state capital with a population of 66,000.

At that time few Brazilian maps depicted Paapiu, but many showed a vast area around it as the indigenous reserve of the Yanomami, among the most culturally intact of Brazil's 180 or so tribes. By reserve rules, all non-Yanomami here were trespassers; in reality, however, garimpeiros treated this land as their own, asked no permissions, paid no landing fees or royalties. The reserve existed only on paper.

Though indigenous lands were ensured by the Brazilian Constitution, the military has long sought to redraw boundaries and carve up the original Yanomami tract into 19 much smaller islands surrounded by non-reserve lands. Even today many "Indian" lands technically have not been legally transferred to natives, or even secured against miners. The same situation plagues many national parks and other federal reserves in Brazil—they are formed by decree, but not backed up with surveys or hard cash. Then garimpeiros come along, generating the hardest of hard cash in this Third World debtor nation; for years evicting them from places like Paapiu was never even considered.

FUNAI, Brazil's federal agency for Indian affairs, is charged with, among other things, ensuring the health of Indians and defining their lands. Critics have called it inept, even intentionally derelict. Its realm is vast. On paper, Brazil's 230,000 Indians own nearly a tenth of the country, more than 300,000 square miles. The agency oversees them with fewer than 5,000 employees, and it lacks an enforcement branch. It can call in federal police but almost never does. FUNAI vice president Airton Alcantara explained, in 1989:

"We do not have the resources to remove all garimpeiros. There are not enough federal police to send to all the invaded areas, and the police don't have money. To remove 100 garimpeiros recently, we had to ask for 18 police agents. Just the state of Roraima has 40,000 miners—only an enormous act by government could remove so many." What about Brazil's well-equipped, well-financed military? Said Alcantara, "Even if we took all garimpeiros out, the next month they'd all be back, or they'd just go someplace else."

Another FUNAI official told me he'd recently counted 33 helicopters on the ground at Paapiu, apart from other airraft. He shook his head, amazed at the garimpeiros' audacity. But had he told his superior or the police? Had the agency responded? Again, he shook his head.

An air of hopelessness pervaded FUNAI, yet Alcantara insisted that indigenous reserves were genuine: "Of course. They are ensured by the constitution."

Although FUNAI had exerted almost no control over miners, it had succeeded rather well at excluding most other non-Indians from indigenous reserves, especially anthropologists. Many of them repeatedly had been denied visits to the very tribes they knew best. Doctors and missionaries also had been barred. Not surprisingly, they detested the agency. A sampling of their comments:

"FUNAI is a revolving door—anyone good always leaves."

"It's very, very corrupt."

"FUNAI is the office boy of the army."

"They are criminals."

"Indians are heroes to survive FUNAI."

Alcida Ramos told me of a nongovernmental group called the Committee for the Creation of the Yanomami Park, or CCPY, which in the mid-1980s provided the Yanomami with doctors and a vaccination program:

"They covered practically the whole Surucucu area, including Paapiu—about 4,000 Indians. In August 1987 the garimpeiros invaded, and the army and FUNAI went in and told the doctors, 'You have two hours to pick up your things and leave.' All of them. Since then, no one has been there to treat Indians. Today Paapiu is a center of malaria epidemics. The Indians are not dying of measles, of tuberculosis, of those things they were vaccinated against. But they *are* dying of malaria. They have all kinds of skin diseases. They are dying for lack of medicines, cheap medicines. Right now."

FUNAI denied Alcida access to Paapiu. But in June of 1989 a congressional commission invited her along on its investigation of the area, thus enabling her to pierce FUNAI's blockade. Her report:

"It was like Vietnam—you couldn't stay three minutes in silence. One plane after another, after another, taking off with an incredible roar; the noise drove you crazy. And then helicopters: up and down, up and down. And the movement of people—prostitutes, garimpeiros with backpacks, all over the place, all the time.

"There was no FUNAI representative there at all. The infirmary was abandoned,

Man-made inferno blackens daytime skies in Brazil, where ranchers have turned millions of acres of forest into cattle pasture, most only marginally productive.

the pharmacy a shambles, with broken glass all over the ground. Syringes were scattered about for children to pick up and play with. It was awful—I'd never seen anything as depressing. The team of photographers with us took photos like crazy. This was what FUNAI replaced the doctors with. And the Indians are dying because of it. It's genocide."

Since Alcida's return from Paapiu, she added, stories of Indian killings had filtered out from the Surucucu area. "But no one knows for sure what's happening, because no anthropologists are allowed in. And that's the idea—to keep it just rumors flying around. A lot of very strong interests want Indian lands and think the Indians prevent progress. Many see the nakedness of the Indians as a major embarrassment, a factor responsible for the underdevelopment of Brazil. They think if they can't get rid of Indians physically, at least they'll get rid of them culturally."

By October 1989 FUNAI still had no representatives at Paapiu. Its pharmacy there, however, was orderly, though scantily stocked. Three young men, neither

Indians nor garimpeiros, had done the work. One wore his dark hair short as an army recruit's, save for a tiny ponytail.

"Hare Krishna," he greeted me with a smile. "H-H-Hare Rama," I returned slowly, stunned. Here, in the middle of the Amazon, just a few yards from the house of the damned, I'd come expecting Vietnam—and found Hare Krishna.

The youth, Datta Dasa by name, was the sect's lone member here; he and his two companions, all idealists, had dropped out of college earlier that year to search for something more meaningful to them than the classroom. In time they came to Paapiu, moved into its abandoned FUNAI buildings, and solicited medicines, food, and other aid from all comers, including garimpeiros and the army. Then, without medical or pharmacology degrees, the trio began dispensing medicines and taking blood samples for analysis in Boa Vista. They also shared the Yanomami's anguish more totally than even they

had expected. All three contracted malaria.

Paapiu's Indians, said Datta, had totally given up. Dispirited by the many disruptions of their traditional life-style, they now relied on others for all their needs. They no longer planted manioc or other crops, and they hunted very little. He showed me *beiju*, manioc cake, he'd learned to make for the Yanomami from tubers supplied by neighboring Indian villages. Baking it had become one of his regular chores. He spoke of the need for vitamins as well as malaria medicines—always in short supply—and castigated FUNAI as "a mafia. They get money yet never spend any on the Indians. Not here, anyway."

Alcantara denied such charges with a blizzard of numbers. Agency income versus outgo. Payroll. Operational expenses. Budgetary demands. But mere figures could not deny the reality of Paapiu.

The case of the Yanomami is only the most recent outbreak in an endless plague of shoddy deals, outright abuse, and annihilation visited upon indigenous peoples. Anthropologists estimate that eight million

Indians occupied what is now Brazil when Columbus arrived; about 230,000 exist today. Eighty-seven Brazilian tribes have become extinct.

And yet in early 1990 a ray of hope: Brazil's outgoing president, José Sarney, ordered garimpeiros to leave Yanomami areas of Roraima. His successor, Fernando Collor de Mello, forcefully carried out the eviction and has threatened to dynamite the airstrips. Collor also appointed a strong environmentalist, Nobel laureate José Lutzemberger, as his minister for the environment. Perhaps equally dramatic changes will come to FUNAI, and the Yanomami's lot will improve.

But Collor's signals remain mixed. He is committed to the military's plan for the frontier, which intends to subdivide Yanomami lands, and his largest plurality during his 1989 election was in Roraima,

Dreams of the good life fuel Brazilians to incinerate great stretches of rain forest (opposite) for cattle ranching (below)— although soils often prove too thin and easily eroded to sustain large herds.

Farming Madagascar's denuded earth, a family plants rice on steeps where trees once stood. Ballooning pressures of a population that has doubled since 1965 mean continued deforestation despite ever-diminishing returns.

which garimpeiros politically control.

Apart from the Yanomami, what of other rain forest peoples? Worldwide, they face extinction—cultural if not physical. Northern Thailand's Hmong, the Pygmies of the Congo basin, Sarawak's Penan, many groups are threatened. Their tragedy affects us all; each tribe's disappearance diminishes the world not only by the loss of human life and culture but also by the disappearance of that rarest of commodities: knowledge.

Says Darrell Posey, "The preservation of native peoples and the preservation of tropical forests are intimately linked. Native peoples know their regions' biological and ecological diversity and how to conserve it. They've been doing that for thousands and thousands of years. But we have not given this traditional knowledge its proper value. Most indigenous forest systems have never even been studied."

Just as the rain forest's lavish diversity has both economic and aesthetic ramifications, so does indigenous knowledge. Tropical peoples discovered curare, quinine, and ipecac. They invented the hammock and devised various uses for rubber. They detoxified manioc. Already their knowledge has benefited the whole world. Might not additional indigenous know-how help us find in nature new medicines, fertilizers, pesticides, growth stimulants, and a host of other beneficial natural products? Many scientists believe such substances, well known to local tribes, already exist in the rain forest and merely await modern man's "discovery" and development.

INPA's Dr. Schubart, for example, considers the Amazon forest "a huge reserve of scientific information for pharmacology, genetics, applied ecology, microbiology—lots and lots of information." Surely marrying such forest knowledge to modern science would give an incalculable boost to what promises to be a major industry of the 21st century: biotechnolo-

gy. The rewards—social and economic—could be awesome.

"Today everyone talks about biotechnology," observes Nikolaus von Behr at FUNATURA, a nongovernmental Brazilian conservation group. "Well, the raw material of biotechnology is genetic diversity. *Nature.* Brazil has it. No developed countries have this great treasure we have. But we are transforming it to ashes. Or to soybeans or something else. The 1990s are the last chance, really, to protect the genetic pool we have."

Schubart notes some positive signs: "Environmental problems are no longer merely for the academic, the romantic, the butterfly collector. There's real concern on the part of the common people, here and elsewhere, over the ecological limitations of the planet."

Von Behr agrees—in part. "Yes, everywhere today ecology is *in.* Margaret Thatcher is now a 'green'; George Bush is an environmentalist. In Brazil people are becoming more interested in environmental matters. This is positive, very positive. But it is not enough—because you don't see the destruction stopping."

Darrell Posey asks, "Why are we cutting down rain forest when we don't even know what we're destroying? Why are we destroying the people who *do* know what is there, which could be worth enormous amounts of money? It makes no sense."

Will we halt the waste? Will we react in time to save the bulk of the earth's gene pool and our invaluable storehouse of indigenous knowledge? Or will we continue to "improve" rain forests much as we have other realms, altering them, often permanently, making them far less wonderful, far less productive, and in fact far less valuable economically? The choice, the world, is ours.

Red tide of mining spoil gradually drowns remnants of a Brazilian forest already ravaged by backhoe and bulldozer as a mining company dredges the region for vast but widely scattered tin deposits.

FOGGY RAIN FOREST, CAMEROON

Saving the Rain

"Will the chitter and hoot of the monkeys be stilled? Will tropical winds one day ruffle only ashes and cinders?"

by
Ron Fisher

Forest

Among the traffic on the Pan American Highway one day in 1988 was a truck rolling north through Panama toward Costa Rica with an unusual cargo: 1,350 iguanas. Dr. Dagmar Werner, whose iguanas these were, was herself a little unusual, a forceful, no-nonsense German biologist moving her operations from Panama to Costa Rica. But at the border there was a problem. Mud slides caused by Hurricane Gilbert had closed the highway to the north, delaying the arrival of Dr. Werner's import permits. Costa Rican customs officials, with no instructions regarding her arrival, refused to allow her or her cargo in.

So Dr. Werner rummaged around in the back of her truck until she found Ignacio, a complacent ten-pound iguana that doesn't mind being held, and hefting him "like a babe in arms" explained to the befuddled officials the point of her studies. Appalled that anyone—especially a lady—would so much as touch a live iguana, never mind *hold* one, the officials debated with her for a while but finally relented and let her continue on her way. But not before calling into question her sanity. "Are you crazy?" one of them asked her. "Or normal?"

Normal in a crazy sort of way, she might have answered, for those were no ordinary iguanas in her truck. They were homely little soldiers in the battle to save the world's rain forests. And Dr. Dagmar Werner—courteous but strong-willed—is no ordinary woman. I met with her in her home in San José, Costa Rica.

"When you talk of saving the rain forests, there are two things you should keep in mind," she told me. "One: Protection of the forests by itself usually doesn't work. Putting fences around rain forests and calling them parks is almost certain to fail, largely because of the second thing you should keep in mind: People are hungry. Many of the countries these forests grow

in are in the Third World, with much of the population living in poverty. It isn't fair for us, in the developed countries, to expect hungry people to ignore livelihoods that can be made from rain forests. But we must find ways to use the forests without destroying them. The best idea I've run into for getting a high-protein sustainable yield from rain forests, simply and economically, is farming the green iguana."

Iguana iguana, long a staple in the diets of Latin Americans, once occurred naturally and plentifully in the region's tropical rain forests, but loss of habitat and pressure from egg collectors and hunters have nearly eliminated it in many areas.

D
r. Werner's scheme is not complicated. She hopes to encourage farmers to raise iguanas in captivity until they are a few months old, then release them into forests; simple feeding stations would help keep the animals nearby. Within two years the iguanas would yield at least as much meat per acre as cattle would. Farmers would thus have an incentive for leaving the forests standing instead of clearing them for cattle pastures. In fact, it would be to their economic advantage to plant more trees.

In an experimental program for the Smithsonian Institution that began in Panama in 1983, Dagmar Werner seemed instinctively to do everything right the first time around. Artificial underground laying nests, which the female iguanas burrowed into, were soon full of eggs; dug up and reburied in Styrofoam ice chests filled with dirt, at least 95 percent of the eggs

Herbarium technician Ekema Stephen Noumbe, of the Limbe Botanic Garden in Cameroon, catalogs a plant on Mount Cameroon. Fern spores (left) dust a delicate pattern on his arm. Botanical gardens and gene banks play major roles in ensuring genetic diversity by preserving threatened species for future generations.

hatched. Within just a few years, Dr. Werner had thousands of iguanas, both in captivity and free ranging like chickens in the surrounding rain forests.

"But when the troubles with Manuel Noriega began in Panama, funding dried up—no one wanted to send money into the country. That was when we loaded the iguanas into trucks and came here to Costa Rica." Initial results in Costa Rica are equally encouraging. At least 30 farmers have expressed interest in raising iguanas.

Dr. Werner is not going to save the world's rain forests single-handedly, but her efforts may prove to be one piece of the puzzle: how to use the forests for the sustainable production of a variety of products and thereby save areas of them.

Many forests are being felled by large corporations for pastureland, for mining, for construction materials—to satisfy domestic needs as well as the demands of developed nations.

Countless trees are being cut for fuelwood for the 1.5 billion people who

Slide show (above) for villagers teaches conservation at the Kilum Mountain Forest Reserve in Cameroon. Alfred Chiateh, foreman of the project tree nursery, rebukes a bird poacher (above, right). A project worker (below) whose shirt shows a Bannerman's turaco, the reserve's symbol, displays confiscated snares and slingshots.

live in the tropics. And the axes and fires of farmers and ranchers are clearing forest for small-scale operations. This destruction is not likely to stop, experts say, until alternative fuels and means of livelihood are found for the people doing the cutting and burning. Impoverished peoples will protect trees only when it is to their advantage to do so.

Awareness has grown in recent years of the threats to the world's rain forests—and the importance of trying to preserve as much forest as possible. Proposals have been floated and efforts launched in a number of countries by conservationists, governments, and concerned citizens. It is difficult to be optimistic, however, about preservation, considering that roughly 50,000 square miles of rain forest are destroyed annually.

Conservation organizations have been at the forefront in alerting the world to the terrible price it is paying for deforestation. The World Wildlife Fund—U.S., known internationally as the World Wide Fund for Nature; the Nature Conservancy; Conservation International; and the International Union for Conservation of Nature are among those which have devoted funds, expertise, research, and legal advice to the battle toward halting the destruction of rain forests.

Celebrities from the entertainment world have also taken up the fight. Rock musician Sting has become identified with the campaign to save the forests, and at the Earth Day 1990 celebration in Washington, D.C., actors Tom Cruise and Richard Gere and and singers John Denver and Olivia Newton–John helped the 350,000 participants focus on the plight of the planet, including the dangers of deforestation.

The mistaken impression sometimes arises that it is up to developed nations to save the rain forests when, in fact, indigenous peoples and local interest groups often are quite sophisticated in the use and protection of the forests.

In Brazil, for example, the Kayapó Indians recognize and use some 600

Reforestation, sustainable forest industries, education, and improved farming practices on nearby lands may save the Kilum Reserve, protected by law since 1987.

species of plants and classify ecological zones in a way that is more detailed than many "modern" systems. They recognize about 15 distinct zones, according to the amount of tree or shrub cover, the presence of water, and the nearness of hills or mountains. In the savanna areas of their territory, the Kayapó manage forest "islands," where most of the plants were set

Whether viewing gorillas in Zaire or birds in Costa Rica, ecotourists bring new sensitivity to tourism and cash to debt-burdened tropical countries—while doing little harm. Tourist fees now pay for guides and guards in Zaire's parks; tourism generates a growing percentage of Costa Rica's foreign exchange.

involved in the planning of parks and preserves on their land. They were concerned that the forest, their home for thousands of years, might be wrested from them.

Half a million rubber tappers, or *seringueiros,* in Brazil have banded together to urge a halt to deforestation and the establishment of protected reserves where they would be licensed to collect latex, a renewable resource.

Another example of local political action comes from Sarawak in Malaysia, where in 1987 several tribal groups barricaded logging roads to protest damage to their land and pollution of their rivers by timber companies. Police arrested the protesters and dismantled their barricades.

Taking the situation of these embattled protestors as emblematic of rain forest peoples worldwide, one must ask how they can ever hope to stave off the devastating incursions of big business, as well as the more insidious encroachment of millions of small farmers and fuelwood gatherers, many of whom live in absolute poverty. Answers, if they come, must arise, of course, from the governments of the nations involved. A role that developed nations might play, if they would, is to help these governments find ways to lighten the burden of their crushing foreign debts.

Only when the whole world, Peter Raven believes—especially those individuals and nations that control the majority of the wealth—realizes that the survival of all of us depends on our willingness to preserve, to use, and to cherish the biodiversity of rain forests will we make any

out by the Indians themselves. They build mulch piles, which they then use to fertilize their crops. They understand crop rotation and frequently visit clearings to gather seeds for planting in old fields and in new forest islands.

And in 1989 a delegation of Amazonian Indians, in feathers and paint, met with environmentalists to ask to be headway toward saving areas of forest.

Some tropical nations, beleaguered as they are, have established parks and preserves as a way of saving pieces of rain forest. Take a chunk of forest, the reasoning goes, make it a park, and charge tourists to visit. But parks that ignore their human neighbors, as well as parks that are not adequately protected, are doomed to fail. The tropics are littered with "paper parks" that do no more than protect ravaged, denuded hillsides and rivers thick with silt.

To be successful, parks and preserves must complement their surroundings and recognize the realities of the world they fit into. The Community Baboon Sanctuary in Belize is an example. It was first established to protect the canopy habitat of the black howler monkey (locally termed a baboon), but now its goals have expanded. Farmers within the preserve have agreed to farming practices that will halt riverbank erosion and speed the recovery of slash-and-burn farmland. The size of the sanctuary has also grown. It now includes an area of 8 villages in 18 square miles along the river.

The Cuyabeno Wildlife Production Reserve, a 630,000-acre area in the northeastern corner of Ecuador, is another successful rain forest park. It enforces strict protection of forest and streamside habitats as well as a Siona–Secoya Indian reserve. Its managers are developing wildlife management projects as well as tourist and educational facilities. It protects an area exceedingly rich in wildlife and culture.

Another biologically lavish and diverse area, in Cameroon, is considered a model for forest parks in Africa. Species-rich Korup National Park shelters nearly a quarter of the continent's primate species. Its plan calls for providing local people with alternative sources of food to discourage hunting in the park; for finding sites for resettling people now in the park; for training and educating a staff; for developing tourism and a scientific research program; and for devising sustainable,

Ghostlike, a tourist passes in a blur down an improved trail in Kinabalu Park, Malaysia. The impact of tourism on rain forests can be slight, conservationists say, if properly controlled and gently managed.

nondestructive uses of the fragile forest.

An important aspect of saving rain forests is the need to preserve the plants and animals found there. According to Raven, a quarter of the world's genetic diversity is likely to become extinct within the next 30 years. As many as 60,000 of the world's 250,000 species of flowering plants may be forever lost—unless representative and ecologically viable samples of rain forest are saved.

Simple preservation often doesn't work. Dr. Calvin Sperling of the Plant Sciences Institute of the U.S. Department of Agriculture explained: "There's a misconception a lot of people have. Here's

a species, they say. We'll just put a fence around it, and we'll have that species preserved. What they often don't think about—or don't know—is that most species are variable. And the variation that might be most interesting is frequently off in an obscure corner."

Dr. Trevor Williams, former director of the International Board for Plant Genetics Resources in Rome, concurs that the problem is a difficult one. "All we can do is protect what we hope are large enough areas to preserve the biodiversity."

A species' downward spiral toward extinction can be halted, but once extinct that species is gone forever. Some zoos and botanical gardens are attempting to preserve endangered plants and animals against the day when habitat might once again be available to them. Although, realistically, only a tiny proportion of the world's vertebrates and plants might be kept from extinction in this way, a number of captive breeding programs around the world *are* sustaining populations of animals—mostly mammals and birds. Other programs are preserving seeds, fungi, and microorganisms for the future.

Unfortunately, there are few well-developed zoos or botanical gardens in the tropics. Huge foreign debts drain limited national resources and are a major contributor to the dearth of such facilities.

Teaching local people new techniques for land use is another method being promoted to save rain forests. In Papua New Guinea, for example, the Shifting Agriculture Improvement Program teaches farmers to use contour mounding and compost and mulch bedding to ease erosion and to plant fruit and timber trees together to inhibit pests.

The tropical forests on the slopes of Mount Oku (or Kilum) in Cameroon shelter several rare or endangered species, and the region's relatively fertile soil sustains large numbers of people as well.

Among the important products of the region is the bark of the *Prunus africana*, or *Pygaeum*, used commercially in the treatment of prostate disease. In recent years this species has been overexploited. Since 1987 the Kilum Mountain Forest Project, sponsored by the International Council for Bird Preservation and the Cameroon government, has developed a program to save the forest and at the same time ensure continued livelihood for local farmers. It combines the establishment of a forest reserve with environmental education, the development of forest industries, and improved farming systems.

Sustainable harvesting of commercially valuable rain forest products may become a primary means of saving significant portions of forest. In the Brazilian Amazon, for instance, the value of rubber and Brazil nuts alone was some 35 million dollars in 1986—not an insignificant sum. Extracting such forest products may help local economies prove self-sufficient, possibly slowing the advance of ranching and logging and providing jobs for the people.

The heightened awareness of the plight of rain forests may improve the marketability of certain products of the forest. For example, Ben & Jerry's, an ice cream manufacturing company headquartered in Vermont, has begun marketing Rain Forest Crunch, a confection made with Brazil nuts and cashews. The company will be buying hundreds of thousands of dollars' worth of nuts a year.

And to fill the demand for tropical hardwoods, alternatives to clear-cutting must be found. The Yanesha Forestry Cooperative in Peru has pioneered a method of sustainable harvesting. Cutting is done in strips about 20 to 50 yards wide, each at least 220 yards from any strip cleared in the previous year. The strips are narrow

Treetop observations reveal secrets of the rain forest canopy. Biologist Donald Perry designed this aerial tramway to survey the plants and animals that live high above the forest floor in Costa Rica.

enough to be revegetated naturally by seeds from the surrounding forest; within a few years they produce a rich regrowth.

Extracting resources from the rain forests while leaving them intact makes more sense than clear-cutting and burning them. Once a rain forest is gone, it cannot be replaced. Restoration can approximate the original forest, but it cannot replace the diversity and complexity of the original. Still, restoration can sometimes speed regeneration and make deforested land productive again. Any forest is better than bare hillsides and eroded gullies.

In Haiti, where less than 2 percent of the country's original forest cover remains, a project funded largely by the U.S. Agency for International Development (AID) has promoted tree farming by supplying farmers with seedlings and support. Each year with the help of the agroforestry project, Haitian nurseries distribute 70 million seedlings to 45,000 small farmers. The seedling survival rate is better than 50 percent, and after a few years the fast-growing trees can be sold as fuelwood and timber. A valuable by-product of the program is the slowing of the soil erosion that has devastated Haiti's hillsides.

A creative program in Ecuador addresses the problem of incentive: how to get poor farmers to spend time and effort caring for trees whose economic benefits they will not reap for years, perhaps decades. Under the plan the government authorizes bank loans to farmers to plant trees. After two years, if the trees have been properly looked after and are growing, the government repays the bank. After 10 or 20 years, when the farmer has harvested his first crop of wood, he repays the government the principal but not the interest. If, however, the farmer neglects the trees and too many die, he pays back the loan with interest and penalties.

And the catalog of ideas goes on. Some are complicated economic schemes; some are as simple as schoolchildren collecting pennies. In Vermont, for example, the Rutland *(Continued on page 183)*

Feisty fulvous bellied antwren makes a reluctant subject for ornithologists studying the avifauna of Brazil (above). In Costa Rica a lepidopterist stalks butterflies at La Selva Biological Station. Increasing our knowledge of the rain forest, scientists say, could help save parts of it.

Taking the plunge for science,
Dr. Claude Gascon of Florida State
University and his assistant
Ocirio de Souza–Pereira explore
amphibian habitat in Brazil.
In a 7,500-acre area, they have
studied 25 species. Among their
subjects: Bufo marinus, *South*
America's largest toad (left).

County Audubon Society has helped fourth and fifth graders contribute several hundred dollars to a campaign to purchase land in Guatemala for parks.

There, as well as in rain forest countries around the globe, ecotourism is growing and bringing hard currency into local economies. If some of this money can be devoted to parks and preserves, it may well help save areas of rain forests. As the world shrinks, tourists look for new destinations and new experiences. Rain forests offer both, with fascinating flora and fauna and new climates and terrains. Already you see the tourists, with their binoculars and cameras, stalking jaguars in Guatemala or leaf monkeys in Malaysia or gorillas in Zaire. I've joined them myself, hunkered down in a flat-bottomed boat in the broiling sun, scanning muddy riverbanks for crocodiles in Papua New Guinea; or bouncing along in a rubber dinghy after sea lions in the Galápagos Islands. Generally tourists are a generous group, spending money freely in their host countries, yet doing little damage.

A complex economic plan for saving

Like "the miraculous offspring of a squirrel and a bird," a researcher wrote of the golden lion tamarin, a monkey now nearly extinct. Zoos breed the animals, train them to live in their natural habitat in Brazil, then release them. A technician (below) fits one with a radio transmitter.

tropical forests involves debt-for-nature swaps. The idea originated with Thomas E. Lovejoy, formerly an official of the World Wildlife Fund and now with the Smithsonian Institution, in a brief 1984 article in the *New York Times*. "The international debt crisis should remind us of the ecological as well as the economic links between rich and poor," he wrote. "Why not use the debt crisis . . . to help solve environmental problems?" The idea was first tried in Bolivia in 1987 and has since been applied in a number of other countries.

Future swaps, Lovejoy thinks, should be on a much larger scale and be undertaken by governments instead of conservationists. "The real problem of debt-for-nature swaps . . . is that they have basically fallen on private organizations to conduct them with . . . limited working capital."

Another problem sometimes overlooked by those promoting debt-for-nature swaps is that the debtor country, as part of the arrangement, must come up with cash. However, when commitments to conservation projects mesh with other local priorities, debt-for-nature financing can serve rain forest countries well.

Here's how it works: Many countries with tropical rain forests have huge foreign debts. If all parties agree, a portion of this debt can be redeemed at a discount and applied to local conservation efforts.

In one transaction American Express sold 5.6 million dollars in Costa Rican debt titles to the Costa Rican National Parks Foundation for $784,000, an 86 percent discount. The money used by the foundation for purchasing the debt came in the form of grants from a wide variety of sources, including the Nature Conservancy. The Central Bank of Costa Rica converted those debt titles into local currency bonds worth 1.7 million dollars and placed them in an endowment fund for rain forest preservation projects. Everybody won something. American Express earned a hefty tax benefit, the Central Bank retired some of the national debt, the donors more than doubled the purchasing power of their con-

tributions, and Costa Rica obtained funds for programs already targeted as national goals by the Ministry of Natural Resources.

Costa Rica—whose name means literally "rich coast"—is an unusual country. Perhaps the most stable democracy in Latin America, it has no army. Its people enjoy the highest literacy rate in the region—and higher than that of the U.S. as well. With lovely, uncrowded beaches on both the Pacific and the Caribbean coasts, Costa Rica attracts an increasing number of tourists each year, and—because of its economic and political stability—many United States citizens are choosing to retire there. Furthermore, Costa Rica is one of the world's leading nations in efforts to preserve rain forests. In 1989 I journeyed there to find out why.

I met first with Dr. Rodrigo Gámez, then presidential advisor in the Ministry of Natural Resources, in his office in San José, Costa Rica's capital. As we talked, rain coursed down windowpanes and black clouds scudded overhead.

"Between the arrival of Columbus and 1940," he told me, "Costa Rica lost a third of its forests; between 1940 and the present, we lost another third. By 1986 Costa Rica was leading Latin America both in the destruction of its natural resources and in their protection.

"By now 27 percent of Costa Rican land is protected," he continued. "Most of the wildlands are devoted to absolute protection of biological diversity, but in the wildlife reserves some extraction of resources is permitted."

And how did Costa Rica get to the position of leading the world in the protection of rain forests?

"There were several factors," explained Dr. Gámez. "For one thing, our first efforts were early enough to do some good; that is, we didn't wait until the forests were all gone before we began trying to save them. For another thing, the people of Costa Rica are well educated; they understand the importance of saving the forests, and we have had their support from the beginning. And because the country is so stable, our politicians—and we have been fortunate in our politicians—have been able to focus on the issue and support it. Finally, we have had considerable support from the international community of nations—both with funding and with expertise."

The future conservation of rain forests may depend indirectly on detailed knowledge of forest plants, animals, and microorganisms and on their interrelationships. So, knowing that it's difficult to save something you don't understand, the world's scientists—especially botanists, biologists, and ecologists—have turned their attention to rain forests.

Many come to Costa Rica to a famous research facility, La Selva Biological Station in the northeastern lowlands. It is owned and operated by the OTS—the Organization for Tropical Studies, an international consortium of more than 40 teaching and research institutions. Adjacent to Braulio Carrillo National Park, La Selva has more than 400 species of trees and an almost equal number of bird species. The station has laboratory and research facilities for all sorts of scientific inquiry, and graduate students and professors from all over the world come for varying periods to pursue their particular specialties.

"Most people in tropical biology come through here," said Larry Dyer, a graduate student from the University of Florida. We were sitting in a laboratory filled with filing cabinets, work tables, and little cups of soil samples. Dyer was at La Selva—Spanish for "the forest"—to study gaps. At first I thought he was talking about an acronym of some sort: GAPS. But no, "A gap is what you get when a tree falls in the forest," he told me.

"When one of these huge rain forest trees comes toppling down, with its load of lianas connecting it to several neighbors, it can make a large hole in the forest canopy. Light comes pouring in. Plants on

the forest floor react in different ways. Some have been waiting for this very thing, and they just take off. Others lose out; they are adapted to shade." "Plants can't run away from a bad site," put in Evan McDonald of Duke University, who was working on the physiological ecology of trees. "They have to cope the best way they can."

I next found David Roberts of the herpetology department of the Dallas Zoo, who was studying the territories of snakes, implanting tiny radio transmitters into two species—*Lachesis muta,* the deadly bushmaster, and *Bothrops atrox,* called locally

German zoologist Dr. Dagmar Werner eyes an iguana named Ignacio, a favored pet and one of thousands of the animals she has raised. Dr. Werner pioneered the farming of the edible iguana—"chicken of the trees"—in Central America as an alternative to slash-and-burn agriculture.

the fer-de-lance—that slither through the Costa Rican forests.

Roberts was excited by a recent arrival at La Selva: an eight-foot bushmaster that had taken up position near a trail and seemed inclined to stay put. That night I walked with David and a couple of others to see it. Our flashlights lighted the slippery path and made huge shadows against the walls of trees. We found the snake coiled near a run made by spiny rats. Waiting. It lay there, frozen in our lights, its head a few inches off the ground. It's the largest New World venomous snake.

"People often recover from the bite of a fer-de-lance," David said, "but almost never from a bushmaster. Still, it makes me angry when people attribute evil, sinister characteristics to snakes," he said. "This snake is not evil; it's hungry."

The next morning I followed David into the forest not far from his office to find a fer-de-lance fitted with a transmitter. He carried a small antenna—very like a miniature of a rooftop TV antenna—and a little box with knobs and dials: the receiver. As we walked, the beeps from it grew loud, then softer, as David swung the antenna. I was walking behind him. "It's easy to forget that the snake you're looking for is not the only snake in the forest," he said, "so watch your step." I was already watching my step. We found the fer-de-lance in just a few minutes, nearly invisible against the base of a tree.

Back at his office, David showed me a chart of its recent movements around a territory of about an acre. His map looked like someone's landscaping diagram, with trees, creeks, logs, the edge of meadows all plotted, and the position of the snake each day connected with straight, dotted

Forlorn and ragged, a one-hectare (2.5-acre) plot of Brazilian forest survives in an area cleared for farming. Researchers hope by studying it—and plots of ten, a hundred, and a thousand hectares—to determine the viability of animal and plant populations in patches of forest.

lines. "Knowledge of a fer-de-lance's territory is all part of the rain forest puzzle," David said.

Miles of trails threaded the forest of La Selva. The trees dripped heavy drops, and dragonflies hovered like helicopters; masses of leaf-cutter ants, each carrying a triangular piece of green leaf, looked like tiny sailboats, all sailing the same stream. In the night, shrieks and whistles came from the forest. Falling leaves the size of dinner plates sounded like trees coming down. Toward dawn the rain came in a deluge, and I remembered roadside speed-limit signs: *VELOCIDAD MAXIMA.*

Spending a few days exploring some of the 30 or so parks of Costa Rica, I found that one thing you can expect of a rain forest is rain. At Monteverde, a cloud forest high in the mountains west of San José, the forest was soggy and green with little puffs of mist floating through it. Hummingbirds flitted and darted. Thunder came in great echoing, thumping rumbles, and the rain came soon after. When it cleared, I stood along a roadside with other tourists, our steaming binoculars to our eyes, watching quetzals trail their long tail feathers from tree to tree. In the forest, orchids the size of pinheads intrigued the amateur botanists. Overhead, a three-toed sloth dangled languidly, upside down. It turned its head—slowly—and regarded us. Someone once said that if the three-toed sloth had one more flaw, it would cease to exist. "They come to the ground only once a week or so to defecate," said Jim, our guide. "That's the only time they're vulnerable to attack. From jaguars, especially."

"Jaguars! No wonder they come down only once a week," quipped Carol Procter, one of the group and a cellist with the Boston Symphony Orchestra.

At Manuel Antonio National Park, where rain forests adjoin the white beaches of the Pacific Coast, it rained in the morning, in the afternoon, at night. When

Devastated Brazilian landscape surrounds Thomas Lovejoy of the Smithsonian Institution, Washington, D.C. Lovejoy originated debt-for-nature swaps: Banks in developed countries reduce the debt of rain forest nations if they use an equal amount of local currency to fund environmental programs.

it wasn't raining, you could see places out over the blue ocean or up in the green mountains where it was. Along forest trails, more sloths sprawled overhead, and white-faced monkeys turned their faces down to peer at me. Big gray tiger herons walked along tree limbs, and turkey vultures on stumps spread their wings to dry. Thin balsa trees leaned out over the beach, summoning up old memories of my model airplanes. A rufous-necked wood rail darted along the trail past a tree whose flared trunk looked like the fins of a comic book rocket.

At Tortuguero on the Caribbean coast, a tree full of howler monkeys awakened me every morning, the rumble and roar of their songs sounding like powerful engines. A walk behind the lodge would bring curious spider monkeys hurrying through the treetops to investigate.

It was the egg-laying season of the green turtles, so one night I joined a small group of people for a walk on the beach. Up from the hissing surf lumbered turtles the size of washtubs. They made tracks like tank treads in the sand. We watched silently as our lights caught them, half buried in their excavations, laying their eggs. The egg-laying and egg-hatching seasons slightly overlap here, so, while some turtles were laying their eggs, others' eggs were hatching. Thus another walk on the beach the following morning revealed the feathery tracks of hundreds of baby turtles running through the sand toward the water.

Before leaving Costa Rica, I journeyed one hot day to Iguana Verde, the site of Dr. Dagmar Werner's iguana farm a few miles south and west of San José. Dr. Werner was in Europe on one of her endless rounds of speech making and fundraising, but recent Princeton graduate Mark Forney, who was spending a few months working for her, showed me around. It was much like a chicken farm—appropriately, for the iguana is jokingly called chicken of the trees. There were wire pens with corrugated roofs and various hatcheries and egg-laying facilities.

And thousands of iguanas, measuring from a few inches in length to several feet.

"Everything we do here has to do with growing bigger iguanas faster," said Forney, as he explained the hatching, rearing, and feeding processes. "There are several points to what we're doing here," he continued, as we strolled among the pens. "One is reforestation. If we can get farmers to start planting trees for iguanas, it would be good for the soil, it would help control erosion, and it would eventually provide trees for wood for human use. And of course it would help save the iguana, which is endangered throughout its range, from Mexico south. Finally, iguanas could provide a sustainable source of food for people. They have been eaten in Latin America for 7,000 years."

I knelt down beside a pen full of the animals. Ugly and dim, they are nonetheless as worthy a part of our planet as anything on it: as precious as the whir of the hornbills' wings, or the fragrant, lazy smoke of a Yanomami campfire, or some rare medicinal plant that might prove invaluable in treating disease—things we may be in serious danger of losing. A rain forest is made up of trees, and each tree is a universe as complex, as engrossing—and as holy—as our own. Will we destroy three-fourths of the world's butterflies before we even learn to name and enjoy them? Will the chitter and hoot of the monkeys be stilled? Will tropical winds one day ruffle only ashes and cinders?

Half the tropical rain forests are already gone, and most of the rest may be gone in 20 to 30 years. Saving respectable pieces of these forests now depends on addressing the problems of overpopulation and economic inequities.

Although family planning is slowing birthrates in the tropics, the population there—estimated at 2.8 billion in 1990—will grow by another billion in this decade alone. Good sustainable forestry and

agricultural practices could advance the welfare of these people while taking some of the pressure off tropical forest areas.

Industrialized nations must band together in an effort to relieve the forces that really drive the engine of tropical forest destruction. And—at grass roots levels— concerned individuals, organizations, and government agencies around the world must continue to tackle the problems.

It was hot there in the sun beside Dr. Werner's caged iguanas. "So you're the creatures who are going to help save the rain forests," I murmured. Frankly, they looked as if they just might do it. Imperturbable and stolid, they blinked their slow, heavy eyes and postured like stuffed toys. Iguanas devote their days almost endlessly to eating and growing. They are the only reptiles that both live in and feed on trees. As such, they are metaphors for the proper, balanced use of their habitat. They consume it but don't destroy it.

Perhaps there's a lesson to be learned from the humble and homely iguana. If we treat our planet with good sense and restraint, we can have our forests and use them too.

Resisting the seemingly irresistible, Amazonian Indians testify at the Brazilian Constitutional Assembly in June 1988, opposing the country's "march to the west." Spreading development encroaches on Indian culture, scars and pollutes the land, and destroys wildlife habitat.

Slow and expensive, reforestation represents a last-resort response to rain forest destruction. Workmen in the Malaysian state of Sabah take seedlings from a nursery and transplant them in a denuded area. Heavily logged since World War II, Malaysia has exhausted its easily accessible forests.

"In a fragment of time, we can reduce the richest, oldest plant community in the world to a sterile mockery of its former self," wrote conservationist Robert Allen. Here in Costa Rica, cleared rain forest abuts Corcovado National Park—mankind's choices for the future graphically portrayed.

Notes on Contributors

Photographer **José Azel** has photographed tropical forests in Zaire for the Society and has contributed to previous Special Publications, to NATIONAL GEOGRAPHIC, and to other U.S. and European magazines.

Since 1966 Senior Writer **Ron Fisher**'s assignments have taken him to a number of the world's hot spots but never before to Central America. "One of our guides in Costa Rica," he remembers, "had fled political turbulence in Nicaragua. Meeting this former forest dweller reinforced my conviction that we won't be able to save the rain forests without also saving the people who live in them."

For this book **Michael Melford** returned to the Costa Rican rain forests he had photographed earlier for *Life*. His photographs have appeared on the covers of *Life, Newsweek,* and *Connoisseur,* and he is a regular contributor to the *Day in the Life of . . .* series.

In 19 years with the Society, Senior Writer **Tom Melham** has drawn numerous wilderness assignments that have helped him combine lifelong interests in natural history, writing, and the outdoors. "Amazonia," he says, "has incredible natural beauty, complex and sometimes explosive human situations, major issues of worldwide concern—all coming to a head *now*. It wasn't my easiest assignment, but it's got to be one of the very best."

Michael Nichols, whose photographs have been published in GEO, NATIONAL GEOGRAPHIC TRAVELER, and NATIONAL GEOGRAPHIC, as well as in his own book on mountain gorillas, hopes that his images of "things that are disappearing" will help make their preservation possible. "My work with the Yanomami Indians in Brazil," Nick says, "was one of my most poignant encounters. They are facing a dilemma with no solution as their culture collides with the 21st century."

Prone to severe bouts of wanderlust, Senior Writer **Cynthia Russ Ramsay** has traveled to all seven continents on assignments for Special Publications. "My journey to Southeast Asia took me to some wonderfully wild rain forests, where the whine of chain saws still does not drown out the songs of the birds. The challenge of the '90s is to preserve such places so that nature's soft, sweet voices will always be heard."

Peter H. Raven has been the director of the Missouri Botanical Garden for the past 19 years. He serves on the Research Committee of the National Geographic Society and addresses audiences worldwide on the consequences of rain forest destruction.

For *The Emerald Realm,* photographer **George Steinmetz** returned to Cameroon where around a campfire he found the same Pygmy guide he had used a decade before. George's photographs have appeared in NATIONAL GEOGRAPHIC and TRAVELER.

Assignments have often led Senior Writer **Jennifer C. Urquhart** to the wilds of North America. During fieldwork For *America's Wild Woodlands,* she found skilled craftsmen and the bounty that temperate forests offer. "The riches I discovered in the world's rain forests," she reports, "promise much more exciting prospects for the future well-being of the planet—if major portions of these lands can be preserved."

Illustrations Credits

Index

Acknowledgments

The Special Publications Division is especially grateful to Dr. Norman Myers, consultant in environment and development, Oxford, England; and to Dr. Peter H. Raven, director of the Missouri Botanical Garden, for reviewing the text and illustrations in this book and for providing expert advice and guidance during its preparation. We would also like to thank Dr. Michael J. Balick and the staff of the New York Botanical Garden, other individuals and organizations named or quoted in the text, and those cited here for their generous assistance: Mark Bovey, Dominique Buchillet, Ibsen de Gusmão Câmara, Jason Clay, Stephen Gartlan, Gary Hartshorn, Patrick Jolly, Oliver Henry Knowles, Sally Love, Dom Aldo Mangiano, David Oren, Voara Randrianasolo, Berta Ribeiro, Edward S. Ross, Fr. Joao Saffirio, George E. Schatz, Duncan and Jane Thomas, Celio Valle, George West, James Wheatley.

For the quotation on page one by Paiakan, a Kayapó leader, we wish to thank both Paiakan and Terence Turner, in whose article it originally appeared in *Cultural Survival Quarterly,* Vol. 12, 1988. And as our source of information for the present location of rain forests (map, pages 16-17), we credit the exhibition: *Tropical Rainforests: A Disappearing Treasure,* Smithsonian Traveling Exhibition Service, SITES 1988.

Additional Reading

The reader may wish to consult the *National Geographic Index* for related articles and books. Of particular interest is *Earth 88, Changing Geographic Perspectives. A Symposium.*

The following books may be of special interest: Lonnelle Aikman, *Nature's Healing Arts;* Edward S. Ayensu, editor, *Jungles;* Catherine Caulfield, *In the Rain Forest;* Julie Sloan Denslow and Christine Padoch, editors, *People of the Tropical Rain Forest;* Adrian Forsyth and Kenneth Miyata, *Tropical Nature, Life and Death in the Rain Forests of Central and South America;* Susanna Hecht and Alexander Cockburn, *The Fate of the Forest;* Norman Myers, *The Primary Source,* and editor, *Gaia, An Atlas of Planet Management;* Donald Perry, *Life Above the Jungle Floor;* T. C. Whitmore, *Tropical Rain Forests of the Far East.*

Library of Congress CIP Data

The emerald realm : earth's precious rain forests / prepared by the Special Publications Division, National Geographic Society.
     p.   cm.
     Includes bibliographical references (p.   ) and index.
     ISBN 0-87044-790-4 (regular ed.). ISBN 0-87044-795-5 (library ed.)
     1. Human ecology—Tropics. 2. Rain forests—Tropics.
     I. National Geographic Society (U.S.). Special Publications Division.
GF54.5.E44   1990
304.2'0915'2—dc20   90-6260
                               CIP

Composition by the Typographic section of National Geographic Production Services, Pre-Press Division. Printed and bound by R. R. Donnelley & Sons, Willard, Ohio. Color separations by Graphic Art Service, Inc., Nashville, Tenn.; Lanman Progressive Co., Washington, D.C.; Lincoln Graphics, Inc., Cherry Hill, N.J.; and NEC, Inc., Nashville, Tenn. Dust jacket printed by Federated Lithographers–Printers, Inc., Providence, R.I.